Harvard
Business
Review

Leader's
Handbook

The Harvard Business Review Handbooks Series

HBR Handbooks provide ambitious professionals with the frameworks, advice, and tools they need to excel in their careers. With step-by-step guidance, time-honed best practices, real-life stories, and concise explanations of research published in *Harvard Business Review*, each comprehensive volume helps you to stand out from the pack—whatever your role.

Books in this series include:

Harvard Business Review Entrepreneur's Handbook

Harvard Business Review Leader's Handbook

Harvard Business Review Manager's Handbook

Harvard Business Review

Leader's Handbook

Make an Impact, Inspire Your Organization, and Get to the Next Level

RON ASHKENAS | BROOK MANVILLE

Harvard Business Review Press

Boston, Massachusetts

The web addresses referenced in this book were live and correct at the time of the book's publication but may be subject to change.

Cataloguing-in-Publication data is forthcoming.

Hardcover ISBN: 9781633693760
Paperback ISBN: 9781633693746
eISBN: 9781633693753

The paper used in this publication meets the requirements of the American National Standard for Permanence of Paper for Publications and Documents in Libraries and Archives Z39.48-1992.

Contents

Harvard Business Review
Leader's Handbook

Introduction

Linda ran marketing for a midsize online retailer and was thriving: her team had helped drive six straight quarters of growth, and she was praised by sales for her strong partnership and performance. Linda was also a member of the company's customer council and well respected by the CEO and other managers.

But she felt stuck in second gear. Her ideas for more innovation were politely listened to in executive meetings, but never seemed to go any-where—"Yeah, interesting concept, Linda, but way too blue-sky right now." She raised her hand for bigger jobs in her company, but repeatedly lost out to more experienced outsiders. She wanted to have more impact and occasionally thought about outside opportunities. But when recruiters called, she wasn't able to picture how she could grab the new job and be successful in it.

Linda was frustrated in her quest for a more significant role but had twinges of confusion and insecurity: "Is becoming a leader some mystical transformation? Do I have to be some Sheryl-Sandberg-in-the-making to fulfill my professional dreams?"

Linda's business school friends, Sam and Natalie, also ten years into their careers, wrestled with similar questions. Both were also eager for more opportunities for leadership but were struggling with the transition.

Sam, known for quick learning and hard work, had risen from fund-raising manager to chief operating officer at a growing community non-profit. "I'm totally jazzed by the work here and have 100 people reporting to me," he told Linda proudly. "But I keep waking up at 3 a.m., wondering if I can do this."

Natalie, a rising tech star in Silicon Valley, was itching to found her own startup. She had good management experience and now also some venture backing and a slate of potential employees eager to join her. But she didn't want to launch the business only to have investors force her to hand it over to a more seasoned executive. She sensed that running an entire company would be a bigger—and scarier—challenge than anything she'd done so far.

Linda, Sam, Natalie: this *Leader's Handbook* is for you. If you're hitting a leadership wall like many midcareer professionals, this book will help you break through. It's also for you if you're an established manager wanting to take your career to the next level or to increase the scope of your current job, if you want to start your own business, or if you just want to generally reach for more impact in whatever you're doing. It's for you whether you're at a traditional company, startup, nonprofit, or government organization, or even looking to lead in a more informal or networked enterprise.

Breaking through to a higher level of leadership will require you to think differently and may even be an identify shift for you. You'll have more privileges but also more risk: your daily actions will be much more exposed. But most of all, this shift will require you to *do* different things. You'll be moving from a role where you're focused on your own learning, collaborating with colleagues, and executing on a direction set by someone else, to a role where success depends more on the direction that you set and mobilizing many other people to get the job done. This book will describe the areas you need to excel and how to build those abilities.

Focus on the fundamentals

Today's world desperately needs more and better leaders. Intensifying global competition, rising performance expectations, and proliferating social and economic problems everywhere have put an unprecedented premium on leadership. Furthermore, organizations continue to change (as always); they are now less hierarchical, more networked, more nimble, and more technology-enabled than a generation ago.

These changes are driving demand for guidance that has resulted in an explosion of books, articles, and other methods for building leadership skills and knowledge. There are thousands of leadership titles available on Amazon, with many more appearing every year. Much of it is helpful, but there's also a growing stream of gimmicky quick solutions flooding and confusing the market.

But despite all the change that swirls around us and the cacophony of advice, in its fundamentals, leadership has not changed: it is still about working with other people to achieve common goals.

Given that reality, we believe the best way for any aspiring leader to succeed and to navigate turbulent times is to tune out the noise and refocus on these fundamentals. By mining the wisdom of the most enduring ideas published in *Harvard Business Review*, our own expertise, and the experience of some of the world's top leaders, this book will cut through the noise and provide you with grounding in those fundamentals so you can break through the kinds of barriers that Linda, Sam, and Natalie are facing.

In doing so, this book will bring you some of the most important research and leadership lessons published in the *Harvard Business Review* in the last four decades. Much has changed over these years, but many areas of leadership have remained consistent. Many of the same time-tested frameworks and ideas apply as much today as they did when they were first published. We describe many of these carefully selected HBR articles in the chapters that follow and list them in a Further Reading section at the end of the book (if you see an HBR article mentioned in the text, you can find more information about it there).

To shape these concepts into the approach we describe in this book, we're also drawing on a combined sixty years of our own collective experience working as thought leaders, consultants, or colleagues with leaders of organizations ranging from *Fortune* 50 corporations, to professional service firms, to nonprofits and startups worldwide. During that time, we've seen hundreds of leaders in action. We've also coached them and partnered with them through transformations, crises, and breakthrough achievements. We've stood side by side with them as they confronted their own shortcomings, grew, and learned.

Last, we interviewed nearly forty working senior leaders who graciously shared their perspectives on the core practices and included many of their insights and stories along the way as well.

Let's begin with some context—by simply defining "leadership." You can't develop and get good at something if you don't understand what it is and why it matters. Once you understand the context, we'll give you a snapshot of what's in the book and how it will help you advance as a leader.

What is leadership?

If you want to become a leader or grow your leadership capability, what does that actually mean?

The term "leadership" has never had a precise definition. For some, it simply means the uppermost segment of an organizational hierarchy. For others, it's a set of competencies that are totally distinct from those of a manager, at whatever level, akin to how professor Abraham Zaleznik described them in a landmark 1977 HBR article "Managers and Leaders: Are They Different?," in which he said that managers tame chaos with controls and process, while leaders thrive on ambiguity, creativity, and discovery in order to spur change. For still others, a leader might be a hero whose almost mythical success feels beyond reach, like Steve Jobs or Sheryl Sandberg. And at the opposite extreme, the term "leader" is also often applied to the star on a kids' soccer team or the more junior manager with a large following on social media.

We believe that just about everyone has some potential for leadership, and that organizations—and society more broadly—win when more people develop relevant skills and take more initiative to solve problems.

For this book, though, we define leadership as:

> *Achieving significant positive impact—by building an organization of people working together toward a common goal.*

Achieving significant positive impact

"Achieving significant positive impact" means creating results such as a major business transformation, growth at scale, or a new offering that moves markets. The kind of leadership we describe is not just running a big project; it's about the scale of the results that you achieve when you do. This book will help you achieve that kind of large-scale impact in what you do by encouraging and enabling followers, and creating more value over time than those followers could achieve on their own.

We want you to aim big and understand what achieving it takes. Our chapters are illustrated with examples of successful leaders who have in some way or other really made a difference in their market or competitive arena (for more on these stories, see the box "More on the cases"). For example, one leader we profile, AIG's Seraina Macia, tells how, in a previous job, she led a transformation of XL's North American Property and Casualty business that generated huge returns for the company. Darren Walker, president of the Ford Foundation, explains how he's been transforming global philanthropy by bringing traditional social justice programs into the digital sphere. Paula Kerger, president of PBS, provides another example of major impact based on dramatically expanding the system's educational offerings to children and local communities nationwide. (For full disclosure, note that we've worked with a number of the leaders we describe in the book in coaching or consulting capacities.)

Of course, CEOs and presidents are not the only leaders that we cite, and we don't want to suggest that they are the only role models that you should emulate or the only ones who can create significant positive impact, particularly since it may be a while before you are running an entire organization. However, the steps that these senior executives have taken and the challenges that they have overcome provide lessons for leaders at all levels and in all types of organizations. For example, even if you aren't at the stage of your career where you're developing strategy for the entire enterprise, you might need to figure out a strategy for growing a particular product or for a particular initiative. Similarly, while you might not have the responsibility for creating a people capability plan

More on the cases

Each of the first five core chapters of this book begins with a true story about how a senior leader made that practice come alive in their organization and how it made a positive difference. You'll read about the creation of a vision for the World Bank, the development of a strategy for public television, the intentional transformation of people's capabilities at the Ford Foundation, the step-up in results at XL Insurance, and the drive for innovation at Thomson Reuters.

We've chosen these cases and other shorter vignettes throughout the book because they showcase what the practices we describe look like at organizations that might have similar challenges to the ones that you work at today or aspire to run tomorrow. We drew the cases from a diverse set of organizations—for-profit, nonprofit, and public sector—that have long-standing track records rather than the latest headline-grabbing firms. Each one shows the power of leaders using that particular practice to create significant impact in the face of tough business conditions, internal resistance, and their own human limitations and concerns. We use these cases to tease out specific lessons that you can apply to your situation, even if your organization is in a different sector or is a different size, or you are in a less senior position.

for your whole organization, you will have to build a top-notch team for your area.

Why "positive" impact?

Emphasizing the word "positive" in our defining phrase about leadership impact is not accidental.

We believe the term "leadership" carries with it a responsibility to create not just any impact, but impact that makes a positive difference toward socially or economically responsible goals rather than a blueprint for effecting some kind of dubious or even evil outcomes. True enough, many of the practices we highlight in this book could be applied to increase performance of criminal or terrorist organizations, too. But we hope you will harness the practices to generally advance people's welfare, and the fair and open creation of wealth and human capital in market economies.

Building an organization of people

Leadership is not about making this kind of impact alone; it depends on doing so through others. Leaders must be masters of building and developing collective work, inspiring and organizing others toward a common goal or goals. Since time immemorial, organizations have been the way that people have coordinated and scaled the effectiveness of human talent. And leaders we have worked with over many years have said that building and motivating an organization is the hardest—and most critically important—part of their jobs.

We use the term "organization" to mean not only traditional corporations like Procter & Gamble or Cisco Systems, but also nonprofit enterprises, startups, divisions within larger companies, government agencies, or even more loosely coupled groups of people operating as informal communities or virtual networks, such as professional associations, social activist alliances, research collectives, and similar. As long as people can be brought together and motivated to work toward a shared goal, there is an opportunity for a leader (or many leaders collaborating) to create large-scale positive impact.

But aligning and motivating that collective effort is deeply challenging. For leaders to succeed, they must address fundamental dilemmas about the human aspects of getting people to work together: differing strengths, attitudes, experiences, ambitions, beliefs, and limitations. And those must be somehow rationalized and aligned with an overall strategy and commitment to achieving collective performance.

For example, Seraina Macia created impact by developing and aligning different groups at XL Insurance, many of whom had conflicting views about how to meet customers' insurance needs. Darren Walker had to shape a new culture and make some tough people choices to shift the Ford

Foundation toward addressing digital justice challenges. Paula Kerger and her team achieved success in transforming children's television by artfully mobilizing the locally owned and operated network of local public television stations around a new strategic set of service offerings.

The difference between leaders and managers

We use the terms "managers" and "leaders" in this book, and like Zaleznik, we don't think they mean the same thing. In our view, what sets leadership apart is the "impact" piece of our definition—leaders are able to have greater impact over time than managers.

But that's not to say that leaders don't need managerial skills or that they don't do the work of management. Early in their careers, leaders need to master basic managerial skills and hone them through repeated application. Eventually, however, they add more of the unique leadership capabilities and ways of thinking. People who don't make the leap will remain managers and continue to contribute. But those who can add leadership abilities to their management repertoire will multiply their value many times over.

As an analogy, consider how great musical conductors have to stay close to—and will often know how to play—the instruments of key soloists in their orchestra. However, they also learn to go beyond their own instrument and bring together the entire ensemble.

FIGURE I-1

The leadership difference

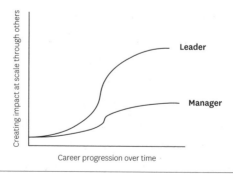

While leadership can be defined differently from management, it also emerges out of it, and when done well, it delivers a leap in impact (see figure I-1). Leaders achieve their difference—their significant impact—by deeply understanding, continuously learning from, and actually practicing management—and then adding unique leadership actions to the mix.

How to develop as a leader: the six practices

If you aspire to become a leader, how do you develop the skills and knowledge it takes? The best way is by live practice—doing and learning on the job. Anyone can and should work on these capabilities beginning in the earliest years of his or her career. We've seen this in our work: that all of the conceptual frameworks, training programs, personal assessments, experiential exercises, and war stories from others begin to truly sink in only when leaders have to apply them in real time, with real people, and real consequences. Of course, coaching, instruction, and reading can be helpful along the way, but there's no substitute for wrestling with, and learning from, actual practice.

In our back-to-fundamentals approach, we have identified six essential and timeless practice areas for aspiring leaders, with each of these constituting a chapter of the book. These represent not an encyclopedia of leadership (see the box "What about soft skills?"), but rather the specific must-do areas that differentiate those who have the strongest impact:

- **Building a unifying vision** (chapter 1). Successful leaders use vision to build and motivate an organization and kick-start innovation and aspirational performance. By setting out broad goals and a picture of success, a vision is the critical first step to achieving distinctive impact through people.

- **Developing a strategy** (chapter 2). After vision, the next step toward major impact is developing a coordinated set of actions so the organization can win—create distinctive value, exceed customer expectations, and beat out market rivals. Leaders do that by

What about soft skills?

As you look at this list of practices, you might wonder why we did not include one about creating a winning culture or a section about the interpersonal aspects of leadership. Aren't these important? The answer is a resounding yes: these softer elements of leadership are *critical* for creating positive organizational impact. Just about every leader we talked to or have worked with over the years has emphasized this view, as does much of the HBR literature.

However, creating culture and building strong interactions with others don't stand alone; they are deeply embedded into all six of our practices. The way that you, as a leader, conduct yourself as you engage in these practices—the behaviors and values that you model and encourage—will have a profound impact on the culture that you create throughout your team, division, or company. But these behaviors are part and parcel of how you go about creating a vision, shaping strategy, getting great people to join you, delivering results, innovating for the future, and growing yourself. As a leader, you are always creating culture. In each practice chapter, we'll highlight ways that you can do this.

At the same time, culture doesn't just happen by itself as an outcome of your behaviors. As a leader, you should be intentional about what you want the culture to be and the extent that you need to change it in some way. There are specific levers you can use to nudge it in the right direction over time. We have included an explicit discussion of how to do this in chapter 3—getting great people on board—because many of the levers involve people: whom you recruit; whom you reward, recognize, and promote; how you measure performance; and how you develop people so that they internalize the values and behaviors that are important to winning. There also is a section on how to create a culture that embraces innovation in chapter 5—innovating for the future.

challenging their enterprise to answer—and then execute successfully upon—critical questions about where and how to compete.

- **Getting great people on board** (chapter 3). Nothing matters more
  to great leaders than people. They recruit, engage, develop, and
  align the members of an organization with a dual proposition: "if
  you can give your all to help us thrive collectively, we'll do our best
  to help you thrive personally."

- **Focusing on results** (chapter 4). Once hired and engaged, the
  people of an organization must deliver the results that will
  create impact. Savvy leaders build the processes that enable people working together to focus on and reach continuously higher
  performance.

- **Innovating for the future** (chapter 5). Winning strategies and performance results are not guaranteed forever. Leaders have to look
  at both the present and the future, and build resilience and creativity into their organizations to keep ahead of changes in markets,
  industry, and business models of competitors.

- **Leading yourself** (chapter 6). Though the collective effort of an organization is needed to achieve impact, leaders themselves are also
  part of that organization. The critical role leaders play demands
  that they also invest in themselves—developing self-understanding,
  ongoing renewal, and enough self-preservation to keep their own
  performance high.

The first five of these chapters follow a logical sequence: leaders begin with
a vision, progressively turn it into action by developing strategy, managing
people, and processes, innovating for the longer term, and so forth.

But these practices are by no means necessarily sequential; they are in-
terdependent, often overlapping, and iterative. For example, vision, strategy, and innovation must be closely related, and you must manage people
and results at all stages of your work. Moreover, the sixth practice (leading
yourself) is foundational to everything else. While it could have been the

first chapter in the book, we chose to end with it, as a way to reinforce the need for leaders to continually learn about *all* of these areas. In addition, we wanted to counter the increasingly common belief that leadership is all about developing inward-facing skills. In our view, leaders need to build their organizations and achieve sustaining results, while simultaneously developing themselves.

Every leader puts their spin on these practices and adjusts them based on their own personalities, proclivities, passions, and situations. But their essence, as captured in the chapters that follow, remains the same.

Practicing the practices

Repeatedly trying, reflecting, and then improving how you apply yourself to create impact through the organization is what's required, and it's why we call these areas of development "practices." Successful leaders constantly do these things and work to improve them.

This journey is different for everyone. It might begin, for example, early in your career, when you're first working as a manager with a more accomplished leader, and joining him or her in doing some of the practices. Over time, you will likely get an opportunity to take charge of some of the practices we describe (creating vision, strategy, etc.). You'll have varying degrees of success as you take these areas on for the first time—that's normal. But by reflecting on your successes and failures at every step, you'll keep making positive adjustments and keep looking for more opportunities to learn.

As you progress, you will reach a level of capability in these six areas that will enable you to achieve increasingly significant value through the people who work for your team, division, or company. As you succeed, these results will begin to build upon one another—you oversee a new product that becomes a runaway hit, or take charge of a transformational initiative that redefines a major market or puts your company on a new path to growth.

As you reach new levels of competency in each practice, you will experience a magnitude change in performance and more followership in your organization, also accompanied perhaps by a growing personal reputation in your industry. More and more people now want to sign up and work with you. Clients or customers ask for you by name. You're invited to represent the company at major industry conferences. Whether you use this momentum to take over a new initiative or to start your own company, you've begun to truly deliver major impact at scale. You've become a leader, capable of rallying an organization of people around a meaningful collective goal and delivering the results to reach it.

A simple map to help you on your way

For a conceptual map of this book, see figure I-2. We treat each practice of leadership distinctly, but as a leader, you're practicing them all at

FIGURE I-2

The six practices of leadership

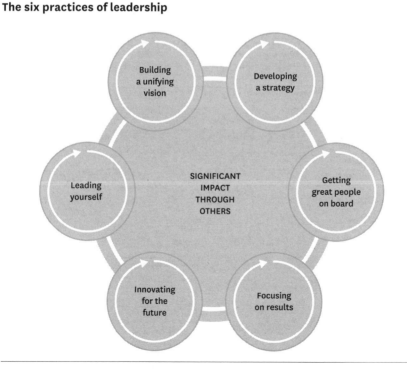

once. You're combining them in the ways that are unique to you and your particular organization and context. And as they come together, you will begin to achieve significant positive impact through others—that's leadership. But it doesn't end there: to keep moving ahead, you will keep practicing, constantly doing, reflecting, and learning to make an impact, inspire your organization, and get to the next level.

So let's get started!

1.

Building a Unifying Vision

A leader's role is to raise people's aspirations for what they can become and to release their energies so they will try to get there.

—David Gergen

Exceptional organizations have an exciting, clear, and simple vision—a vision that honors and reinforces the core purpose of the organization, but also creates a picture of where the organization is heading and what it aspires to accomplish in the future. Consider, for example, DuPont's vision, "to be the world's most dynamic science company, creating sustainable solutions essential to a better, safer, healthier life for people everywhere"; or Facebook's, "to give people the power to share and make the world more open and connected." Divisions and teams within organizations also have visions; for example, Nest, the smart-home division of Alphabet (the parent of what was originally Google), has a vision of creating "the thoughtful home: A home that takes care of the people inside it and the world around it."

The practice of crafting a vision is a key component of your ability to create significant impact as a leader. Whether you are in charge of the whole organization or just a piece of it, a vision provides the starting point for developing strategic plans, recruiting talent, setting goals, and challenging people to find new and better ways to get things done. Equally important, the vision helps to align groups and individuals (who may be doing quite different work) around a common direction, while also inspiring them to contribute to something that is bigger than them.

Your role as a leader is to shape a compelling vision to fit your organization (or unit, or team) and its environment, and then recraft it periodically as conditions change. By crafting, sharpening, or revising your vision in the right way, at the right time, you can have enormous influence over your organization's or unit's direction and the emotional engagement of your people. But this kind of vision doesn't just drop out of the sky. The practice of making a vision is challenging because:

- It can be hard to determine whether it's the right time to develop a new vision; you don't want to do it too often and risk burnout, or not often enough and risk complacency.

- It's easy to be too timid in setting a vision; to do its job, a vision must be bold.

- Many of your colleagues and constituents will have competing ideas and points of view and you'll need to corral these into a coherent direction.

- The process can be time-consuming, so you'll have to carve out time to focus on creating the vision while dealing with shorter-term issues that will seem more urgent and compelling.

- Assuming you are not the CEO, you'll need to connect the vision for your specific team or business unit to your company's overall vision, without losing the overall energy and meaning of the broader vision. Sometimes this is just a smaller version of the corporate vision, but it can be supportive while somewhat different.

Tackling these challenges head-on is a critical part of stepping up from management to leadership. And although it doesn't have to be the first thing you do, you will have to focus on building a unifying vision periodically because it provides the foundation for many of the other practices that will make you a great leader. If you practice it on a relatively small scale with your team or your department, it will give you more confidence to build a broader vision at another point in your career.

As part of this practice, leaders need to first understand what a good vision is; they then need to lead a process for determining the vision for their organization or unit. To give you a sense of what this means, let's look at how Jim Wolfensohn shaped a new vision for the World Bank as a whole and how other leaders in the Bank then built exciting visions for their own teams as a result.

Creating a vision for the World Bank

When Wolfensohn became president of the World Bank in 1995, he inherited a venerable institution under siege. The organization had been successful in supporting worldwide economic development after World War II and promoting democratic social and economic systems during the Cold War. But with the fall of the Berlin Wall in 1989, suddenly the West had won and the quasi-political purpose of the World Bank no longer made sense. Additionally, the opening of world financial markets and the rise of China and other Asian economies meant that developing countries had access to capital from sources other than the World Bank. Meanwhile, the Bank was being criticized for earlier neglect of such concerns as the environment, local culture, corruption, social justice, and others. By the time Wolfensohn took the helm, these forces had coalesced into a public movement, called "fifty years is enough," that explicitly questioned the World Bank's need to exist.

These attacks caused internal morale to plummet. In addition, an internal Bank study had just concluded that one-third of the Bank's projects were not producing the desired economic results.

Given this crisis of confidence, Wolfensohn realized that he needed to reestablish a compelling vision that would support the continuation of the Bank and reenergize the staff. "Reconstruction" and "strengthening the Western Bloc" were no longer relevant, and the core purpose of broad "economic development," while still important, was too vague to resonate with staff at a personal level or the outside world. Something else was needed.

Based on active discussions and debates with his senior staff, Wolfensohn decided that the answer was to refocus the Bank on poverty reduction, an area that an earlier president, Robert McNamara, had first emphasized, but that had become overshadowed by years of debt crises, structural readjustments, and other development issues. After all, in 1996 poverty was endemic, with more than 28 percent of the world's population living in extreme poverty (less than $1.90 per day, according to the World Bank's data). Remedying that dismal reality was an urgent need.

Wolfensohn realized that he couldn't simply cook up a vision for the Bank with his senior team and then drop it on everyone. Instead, there had to be a process of dialogue with stakeholders—listening and testing in a way that would make them feel that the vision was something that they had helped create. To do this, he asked Caroline Anstey, his head of communications, to draft an initial vision statement that would capture his intent to focus the Bank on poverty reduction and then to engage multiple stakeholders in fleshing it out. The team used the initial draft to solicit input from clients, government officials, board members, and senior managers. It held focus groups with staff and built group discussions into various meetings, off-sites, and leadership events. Wolfensohn himself actively participated in many of the sessions and regularly reviewed the emerging vision with Anstey and others.

The result was a phrase that was eventually chiseled in stone on the walls of the Bank's headquarters building in Washington, DC: "Our dream is a world free of poverty."

The stakeholder discussions also generated many other messages about the organization's aspirations, so that the overall vision eventually looked like this:

Our dream is a world free of poverty.

- *To fight poverty with passion and professionalism for lasting results*

- *To help people help themselves and their environment by providing resources, sharing knowledge, building capacity, and forging partnerships in the public and private sectors*

- *To be an excellent institution able to attract, excite and nurture diverse and committed staff with exceptional skills who know how to listen and learn*

Over time, with regular repetition and use, this statement and the aspiration it described became an antidote to the external criticism that called for the end of the Bank. It also helped leaders in the organization to focus and prioritize the Bank's strategic goals, both at the corporate level and throughout the regions, countries, and technical networks in which it operated. Indeed, the focus on poverty alleviation eventually became an ongoing measure of progress, not only for the Bank, but also for other development institutions such as the United Nations. The vision also resonated with the staff at a personal level since many Bank staff either came from poor countries or frequently traveled to areas that were economically disadvantaged.

The power of the World Bank's vision was not just a matter of framing strategy and building engagement, however. It also was unifying, allowing the Bank to leverage the contributions of its individual employees at scale. The Bank, like most organizations, consists of people with a wide variety of skills and backgrounds across many functions. There are economists, agronomists, water experts, civil engineers, accountants, clerical personnel, writers, administrative assistants, and many more, all in different silos, departments, and locations. But because the organization's "world free of poverty" vision was so powerful, these individuals with their unique contributions could feel as if they were joining forces to achieve that larger inspirational goal together. They weren't just writing reports, doing studies, or making loans, but were part of an institution and a team that were striving to make life better for millions of people.

This vision also cascaded through the organization. Leaders of regional divisions and functional areas throughout the World Bank developed visions that catalyzed their people around particular challenges relating to poverty elimination. For example, Mieko Nishimizu, the vice president of the South Asia region, focused on a vision for reducing poverty at the village level in her countries, particularly since many of the previous economic development projects had not reached the villages. Dennis Whittle, another senior leader who headed up a strategy team, developed a vision of leveraging ideas worldwide to fight poverty rather than just relying on the Bank's expertise. This led his team to create a global "development marketplace" for poverty-reduction solutions that eventually became a regular part of the Bank's strategic approach.

What is a vision?

Before we describe how you as a leader create a vision for your department, team, or unit, we need to explain what a vision really is—and what features make it work in all the ways that the poverty-elimination vision Wolfensohn helped engender worked for the World Bank.

"Vision" often means different things to different people; in organizations, it's often confused with "mission," "values," and more. These concepts overlap somewhat, but we believe that vision gives you a unique opportunity to exert your leadership. It is the one pillar that you, as a leader, can periodically reassess and reshape, as Wolfensohn did at the World Bank. Nobody else can do this for you; it's your role to catalyze and steer both the process of determining a vision and also the particular boldness of your approach.

So how is a vision different from a mission or a company's values? An organization's mission is its long-term, mostly unchanging charter—its unique reason for existence. For the World Bank, the mission is to provide financial and technical support for economic development in disadvantaged parts of the world. A network of hospitals might have the mission of "providing a full range of health-care services to a target market," or a manufacturing concern in business might be "to develop, produce, sell, and service certain products for small and medium-sized enterprises." These kinds of statements define the business they are in and can be accessed in their legal articles of incorporation, founder's early statements, or discussions with board members and senior leaders.

Values too are enduring, though they may respond a bit to the times. These are the ground rules for how the enterprise and its people should work to get things done. Values tend to be more personal; they are the ideal operating guidelines for personal behavior that individuals are supposed to follow as they do their work. At the World Bank, for example, a code of conduct called "living the values" outlines specific ways that staff should interact with colleagues, clients, civil society, and local communities, and how managers should ideally behave toward their people.

A vision, on the other hand, is a picture or snapshot of what the organization or your unit wants to accomplish over the next several years or where its efforts are pointing it in the long term. The vision conveys a direction—not how to get there (that's strategy), nor the immediate measurable goals that drive performance, but a context within which specific strategies and goals can be framed. For the World Bank, the shift to freeing the world from poverty represented a material change from the organization's previous direction of facilitating post–World War II reconstruction and supporting Cold War–era democratic capitalism. And at the unit level, Dennis Whittle's vision to leverage ideas from around the world that could reduce poverty was a dramatic change from the strategy team's previous reliance on its own experts. (Table 1-1 shows how vision is different from mission and values.)

To be sure, different leaders approach the term "vision" differently. See the box "The elements of a vision" for another classic definition of how these ideas fit together and what makes an effective vision.

TABLE 1-1

Mission, values, and vision

	Mission	Values	Vision
What it is	Reason for organization's existence	Operating guidelines for how organizational members behave	Aspiration of what the organization wants to accomplish; gives individuals a connected sense of purpose
Time frame	Enduring	Enduring but with specific emphasis depending on the times	Refreshed and revised as the environment changes
Style	Legalistic	Clear and descriptive	Emotional and simple
How it is used	Provides criteria for determining whether to engage in certain lines of business or markets	Provides basis for discussion of personal performance and deciding on ambiguous ethical situations	Provides the context for strategy and goal setting

The elements of a vision

In their classic HBR article "Building Your Company's Vision," Jim Collins and Jerry Porras suggest that your enduring mission and your aspiration are the two elements that meld together to form your vision. Based on their research about organizations that are "built to last," they say,

> A well-conceived vision consists of two major components: core ideology and envisioned future . . . Core ideology, the yin in our scheme, defines what we stand for and why we exist. Yin is unchanging and complements yang, the envisioned future. The envisioned future is what we aspire to become, to achieve, to create—something that will require significant change and progress to attain.

Putting these two elements together, they explain, requires that you "understand the difference between what should never change and what should be open for change, between what is genuinely sacred and what is not."

At the World Bank, for example, supporting economic development through loans and technical advice is the unchanging yin that says why the institution exists, while "a world free of poverty" is the yang, the envisioned future.

What makes a vision compelling?

It's not enough just to set a direction. A vision has to have certain characteristics to be an effective motivator and strategic unifier.

A good vision is aspirational, almost dreamlike, simple, and compelling. It's the kind of statement that should make you want to be part of the organization, to join in the pursuit of that vision. It has emotional resonance. The vision also must be clear: if it's confusing or vague, nobody will follow it. Finally, it must be bold: you must push your organization to look to the future, see around corners, and point toward something audaciously far in front of it.

See the box "Criteria for organizational vision" for a checklist of these criteria to use as you work on your vision.

Criteria for organizational vision

- Conveys a picture of the future
- Bold
- Simple and clear
- Emotionally compelling
- Aspirational
- Provides context for strategic planning

Other vision examples

For the formal vision statements of a range of other real companies, see table 1-2.

TABLE 1-2

Vision statements

Alcoa	At Alcoa, our vision is to be the best company in the world—in the eyes of our customers, shareholders, communities and people. We expect and demand the best we have to offer by always keeping Alcoa's values top of mind.
Bimbo (Mexico)	To be the world leader in the baking industry and one of the best companies in the international food industry.
General Motors	GM's vision is to be the world leader in transportation products and related services. We will earn our customers' enthusiasm through continuous improvement driven by the integrity, teamwork, and innovation of GM people.
Kraft Foods	Help People Around the World Eat and Live Better.
IKEA	The IKEA vision is to create a better everyday life for the many people. We make this possible by offering a wide range of well-designed, functional home furnishing products at prices so low that as many people as possible will be able to afford them.
Nike	To bring inspiration and innovation to every athlete* in the world. *If you have a body, you are an athlete.
Robert Bosch Corporation	Invented for life. Our vision is to enhance the quality of life with solutions that are both innovative and beneficial.
Zappos	One day, 30% of all retail transactions in the US will be online. People will buy from the company with the best service and the best selection. Zappos.com will be that online store. Our hope is that our focus on service will allow us to WOW our customers, our employees, our vendors, and our investors. We want Zappos.com to be known as a service company that happens to sell shoes, handbags, and anything and everything.

The World Bank's vision of "a world free of poverty" has all of those characteristics. It's simple, compelling, and highly aspirational, and it allows the Bank's leaders to set strategic goals, subgoals, and priorities for projects, regions, countries, and the institution as a whole. See the box "Other vision examples" for more visions at both organizational and unit levels.

But not every leader has the opportunity to create a vision as far-reaching as those of these large corporations. The vision you create for your unit, however, should still be powerful for you and your team and should make all of you feel that what you are doing is more than just a job. So no matter what kind of organization you are a part of, think about how your team or unit can have a transformative (or extremely positive) impact on your internal or external customers. (See table 1-3 for some examples.)

TABLE 1-3

Vision statements for small businesses and divisions within larger companies

Lending department of a bank	Our vision is to give our customers the financial means to realize their dreams.
Automobile dealership	We aim to help families enjoy the experience of traveling together.
Internal audit unit of a media company	We want to make sure that our colleagues stay out of trouble and find new opportunities to improve their operations.
Startup solar company	Our vision is that our customers will produce more electricity than they consume.
Warehouse for a manufacturing company	We strive to get the right materials to the right place at the right time at the right cost.
IT department of a pharmaceutical firm	We aim to give our colleagues the tools that allow them to increase the world's health.

Boldness

Vision isn't about just doing incrementally more than what you do now. Rather it's about defining a direction that is significantly different to create new value for the organization and its constituents—not tomorrow but over many years. As Dominic Barton, the global managing partner of McKinsey, told us, "Managers take care of the railroad tracks that are already there and make sure that the trains run well. But leaders shift the tracks, they ponder different futures, they swing for the fences."

This boldness is important because it is what inspires, what serves as a North Star for people throughout your organization. Jim Collins and Jerry Porras describe what they call BHAGs, or "big, hairy, audacious goals":

> *All companies have goals. But there is a difference between merely having a goal and becoming committed to a huge, daunting challenge—such as climbing Mount Everest. A true BHAG is clear and compelling, serves as a unifying focal point of effort, and acts as a catalyst for team spirit. It has a clear finish line, so the organization can know when it has achieved the goal; people like to shoot for finish lines. A BHAG engages people—it reaches out and grabs them. It is tangible, energizing, highly focused. People get it right away; it takes little or no explanation.*

Consider the vision of the MD Anderson Cancer Center in Houston, Texas. Its vision is "to make cancer history," which has the double meaning of developing breakthrough science (historical new discoveries) and eradicating cancer altogether. It resonates with researchers, clinicians, and ancillary workers, as well as donors, patients, and family members. It's also memorable and vivid—and certainly bold. Its boldness has spawned more than a dozen specific moon-shot programs in different clinical departments to make significant advances in reducing mortality and suffering on specific types of cancers in defined periods of time.

Of course, your team may not have a vision at the scale of eradicating cancer or eliminating global poverty, but to be effective, a vision must still be significant relative to the day-to-day work of the team. At AIG, for instance, Seraina Macia currently runs a unit called Blackboard Insurance that is seeking to improve commercial underwriting by developing artificial intelligence and data analytics to reshape the whole process and, by extent, the industry itself. Similarly, the human resource team of a large corporation that we know formulated its vision around making the company one of the top five places to work in the United States and a preferred destination for graduates of engineering schools.

For the most compelling visions, going bold doesn't mean financial success, but rather striving for an exciting contribution to customers or to society. In the HBR article "Successful Startups Don't Make Money Their Primary Mission," describing successful new ventures, Kevin Laws, COO of AngelList, argues that if the goal of an organization is simply to make money, it won't make it through the rough patches. Sure, it needs to make money in order to achieve its vision, but without that separate vision to guide and inspire the people involved, the organization won't do either. Examples of this abound: Google didn't set out to become a company with one of the largest market capitalizations in the world, but rather to "organize the world's information and make it accessible to everyone." Apple didn't start out with the vision of having an astronomic stock price, but rather, in Steve Jobs's original formulation, to "make a contribution to the world by making tools for the mind that advance humankind."

The vision cascade

Note that visions and associated BHAGs are not the sole province of the CEO and the corporate level. Like Macia, if you are the leader of a unit, division, or even a team, you can develop your own bold vision. But for that kind of vision, there is an additional criterion: it must support and align with the organization's overall vision.

For example, Macia's Blackboard unit at AIG is focused on underwriting, but it aligns with and supports the overall vision of the company to leverage technology and data science in the reinvention of insurance. Similarly, the MD Anderson moon-shot programs are essentially visions created by clinical division heads, but they all support the overall vision of "making cancer history."

Whether you are creating a vision for your whole organization or recrafting a vision for your particular unit, keep these definitions and requirements in mind. They'll help you refine and improve your vision—and help your team do the same—throughout the process.

Crafting your vision

You can break the practice of actually crafting a vision to meet these standards into four sequential steps. The first is to determine whether it's even the right time to create or revise your organization's or team's vision. The second is to establish your own draft vision as a starting point. The next step is to engage your own team and other stakeholders in actually crafting a more refined vision together. Finally, you'll need to help your people connect their work to the vision so that they understand how their contribution makes a difference.

Step 1. Determine whether the time is right

Whether you are a CEO or the leader of a department, function, or plant, you need to periodically ask yourself whether you have the right vision for your organization and whether it's time to modify it or work on a new one. That's all the more necessary if you're just coming into a new leadership role.

But, often, particularly for new leaders, there is so much going on and so much to do, it's easy to get caught up in the day-to-day activities and forget or put off setting direction.

Even long-serving executives can become too passive; having been in the same organization for a while often makes leaders blind to their changing environment—at least until some crisis shakes their world and sinks their numbers. But staying attuned to the ways the world is changing is critical for a leader. It is your opportunity—and your role as a leader—to identify when to reshape a vision.

When to develop a new vision

It may be obvious that you need to sharpen or reshape your vision completely because of a changing environment or new organizational opportunities, as was the case with the World Bank. Or it may simply be clear that the current path isn't working.

But the need for a new vision may not be immediately obvious. For example, when Patrick O'Sullivan became the CEO of Eagle Star Insurance in the United Kingdom, the company's senior leaders told him that the company was doing fine and that its vision to provide reliable, low-cost property and casualty insurance was sufficient. When O'Sullivan dug into the numbers, however, he realized that the current business model wasn't working and that Eagle Star was surviving only because it was understating its reserves and was covered from market pressures by its parent company, British American Tobacco. As a result, O'Sullivan spent his first few months meeting with his direct reports, other managers, and groups of employees to help them appreciate the so-called burning platform. As people began to realize the gravity of the business situation, he was able to discuss with them a fresh vision for the company around the concept of "winning through customer service." Eventually this led to a major turnaround of Eagle Star and its subsequent sale to Zurich Financial Services.

Another trap to avoid is what Collins and Porras call the "we've arrived syndrome." This is when your unit or team has had a spectacular achievement—you've really accomplished your aspirational goal, but you haven't replaced it with something new. The temptation for the team (and for you) in this situation can be to look backward at how exciting things were rather than looking forward. If you're not careful, a sense of complacency can set in, and you miss the next threat or the next competitor on the horizon. Overcoming this syndrome requires the development of a next new challenge, a new vision and aspiration.

For example, Intuit spent twenty years achieving the vision of changing the way people managed their personal finances and, in the process, became a software powerhouse, with Quicken as its flagship product. Once it got to the summit, however, other companies started to copy its success, moving into the market and finding new ways of attracting customers. When Brad Smith became CEO in 2008, he recognized that the company had become so focused on adding incremental features to improve usability that it had no big aspiration for the future. So he worked with his team to develop a new vision of becoming "one of the most design-driven companies in the world," moving the organization toward thinking about *delighting* customers. This new vision led Intuit to design products differently, incorporate new skills, sell off legacy products (including Quicken), and rethink many of its ways of working.

Finding the capacity to do this isn't easy, particularly since most leaders already are starved for time. Carving out additional time to devote to vision is hard and can easily be put off until later. So set aside a particular time each year to reflect on your vision and think about whether it still fulfills its purpose. For example, Gary Wendt, the former CEO of GE Capital, used to ask all his business leaders to conduct "dreaming sessions" with their teams each year in advance of the strategic planning process. Each team had the opportunity (and the luxury) of stepping back and dreaming about where the business could be in a few years and how it could be significantly different and better, which would then force the team to assess whether the current vision would get it there.

When to stay the course

Don't be too fast to reset your organization's path. Many visions will last for years and don't need to be changed significantly. The amount of time and work it takes to create a vision is significant—and can actually be destructive if you are pivoting too quickly—so it might be that all you need to do is make sure that everyone understands it.

If you do want to retain the existing vision, at least for now, convey your decision to your team and the organization. Often, new leaders feel that they have to make a big splash and reshape their unit's or company's vision right away, or others may expect them to do so. But since the vision is an aspiration that requires years to achieve, it is perfectly legitimate to say that it's still the right direction but "we're not there yet." Then you can focus your energy—and everyone else's—on what's needed to keep moving forward, pick up the pace, or go about achieving the vision in some new ways. The key is to be explicit about your decision and not leave people guessing or wondering when the big announcement will come.

Finally, even if you and your team *are* convinced that you need new vision, that might not be the first thing you do as a new leader. Sometimes there are more urgent issues to tackle, particularly relating to the survival or stabilization of the firm. Louis Gerstner, the former CEO of IBM who took over the company in the early 1990s when it was experiencing a major financial crisis, is famously misquoted for saying, "The last thing IBM needs is a vision." This was considered a startling comment from a prominent senior leader who had previously been a consultant at McKinsey and was famous for his visionary and strategic acumen. What he really said was that "the last thing IBM needs *right now* is a vision." Gerstner helped IBM refashion its vision as a hardware provider to a provider of integrated solutions. But he started that process in his second year after first dealing with cash flow problems, getting the right leadership team, and redesigning the structure of the company at the beginning of his tenure.

How to gauge whether you need a new vision

To understand whether your organization needs a new vision, first assess the current vision. Is there one? Does it meet the criteria laid out for a good vision earlier in this chapter? (See table 1-4, "Is it time to create or refine your company's vision?" for more questions to ask.)

If you are interviewing for a new leadership role, you should ask each person you talk with to describe the vision, not just for the company, but also for the unit that you might be leading. That's a quick way for you to learn whether one really exists or whether you need to change it. In some cases, it will be obvious, because of either performance shortfalls or a crisis—and that may be why you are being hired. In other cases, however, you may see the need for a new vision, but others may not.

Even if you're not new to your organization or position, you should periodically test whether everyone truly understands the vision by talking to a random sample of people in your organization or department—say, fifteen to twenty. Ask each to quickly share their view of where they think the organization is heading over the next few years and how they feel about it. If you get many different answers or the answers aren't convincing, then perhaps it's time to get to work on a new or refreshed vision. You should also periodically ask yourself and your team whether there have been significant changes in the business environment, technology, or competition that should trigger a rethinking of the vision.

TABLE 1-4

Is it time to create or revise your company's vision?

	If the answer is yes	If the answer is no
Do we already have a clear, compelling, and unifying vision of what we want the organization to achieve in a few years? Can I articulate it? Do other people refer to it regularly?	Congratulations. Keep reinforcing the vision and working toward its realization.	Consider whether the vision needs to be created or improved or whether it needs to be communicated more effectively.
If I asked 25 people at random about the vision of this organization (or this unit), would they give me more or less the same answer?	Congratulations again. You not only have a vision, but everyone knows what it is.	The vision needs to be communicated more effectively.
Are people excited about the vision of what we are trying to accomplish as an organization and of working here? Do they have a sense of purpose that gives meaning to their activities?	This is even better. Your people not only know the vision, but are also excited about it.	This is a signal that you have work to do. You'll need to engage your people so that they can connect emotionally to where the organization is heading.
Has the business or competitive environment changed significantly? Are there new competitors with different business models? Are we no longer able to attract the best and brightest people?	This is also a signal that work may be needed on the vision, and that you'll probably need to engage other stakeholders (e.g., customers, suppliers).	You're probably in a relatively stable environment (unusual these days), and maybe you don't need to focus on changing or modifying the vision. But don't get complacent. Keep monitoring what's going on.
Can we connect the dots between our mission, vision, and values (or operating behaviors)?	Being able to tell a complete story with all of these pieces is very powerful. You're in good shape	Try to put the different pieces together into a story that can be conveyed simply and easily.

Step 2. Develop your starting-point vision

Once you determine that it is time for a new or revised vision, you need to put together a draft starting point to set the process in motion and to convey your perspective on what to include. This doesn't mean that you need to be the sole visionary for your company or your part of it, but at the same time, you can't be absent from the process and just give your vision team a blank sheet of paper.

Based on extensive surveys of thousands of working people in organizations, professors James Kouzes and Barry Posner, in their HBR article

"To Lead, Create a Shared Vision" have found that the ability to be forward looking is the second-highest characteristic of what employees look for in a leader (trailing only behind honesty). In other words, your followers—the people you lead—are expecting you to envision, anticipate, and set a direction for the future. Depending on where you are in the organization, this can mean different things. At lower levels, it could center around articulating a new way of getting projects done faster and with greater impact, or significantly ratcheting up service to customers; at higher levels, it might involve setting direction for how your unit will make a difference in the next few years; and at the CEO level, the challenge will be to figure out an exciting enterprise path for the next decade.

To do this, Kouzes and Posner strongly suggest that you start by talking to and listening to your own people, both direct reports and other followers. Find out their ideas, dreams, thoughts, hopes, and concerns about the future for your team, unit, or organization. Tap into their aspirations and find out what would be exciting for them so that the vision you eventually create will resonate with the people who have to make it happen. See the box "A vision-creating exercise" for one way to do this.

Of course, you can't stop there. You also need to incorporate your own thoughts and dreams. Some of the vision should be based on good common business acumen and insight. Scan the horizon. What's happening in your industry or your sector? Are there unmet customer, market, or societal needs that your organization or unit has the capability to fulfill? Are there new technologies that you could leverage? How could you differentiate your organization from your competitors (or even from other units in the company)? More personally, what's the impact that you'd like to have over the next few years or more? What would make you feel like you've really made a difference?

As you go through this thought process, start putting together options, choices, and what-if statements. For example, when Jim Wolfensohn was first thinking about the vision for the World Bank, he considered the possibility of focusing on measures of global economic development or aiming for a certain number of countries to achieve a target level of financial

A vision-creating exercise

One way to tap into your team members' ideas about vision is to ask them to reinvent their official job titles so that they reflect the kind of value that they want to create and the impact that they aspire to have on customers. Professor Dan Cable from the London Business School, in his HBR article "Creative Job Titles Can Energize Workers," describes how job titles improve employee satisfaction and engagement by giving people a better sense of how their work creates value and impacts customers. Disney is a prime example of this approach—calling theme park employees "cast members" and engineers "imagineers." These titles are consistent with the company's overall vision, which is "to make people happy."

Lior Arussy, founder and CEO of the customer experience firm Strativity, uses this approach to help teams get excited about what they can potentially accomplish together, which is the essence of a team's vision. For example, members of a sales team came up with titles such as "director of customer first impressions," "customer dreams fulfillment manager," and "red carpet roller." All these indicate how the team wants to make customers feel special in their interactions with the company, which is a great basis for a team vision. (For more, see Arussy's book *Next Is Now: 5 Steps for Embracing Change—Building a Business That Thrives into the Future.*)

health. Eventually he settled firmly on the elimination of poverty. This was partly because of what he had heard during his trips to villages and neighborhoods in developing countries about unmet needs and decades of government inaction. But the decision also came from his own deep-seated conviction that the world could be a better place and the value that he put on improving individual lives. In other words, his starting point was not only intellectual, but was also shaped by his personal values.

As you think about creating a first draft vision for your organization or unit, think about how you can respond to the business issues but also be true to yourself. Consider, for example:

- What values and beliefs do you hold broadly and also specific to the mission of your organization or the work of your unit?
- How will your leadership values and beliefs actually shape the organization or your unit for the better?

Once you settle on a focus or theme for your draft vision, also consider how to be bold, audacious, and inspirational. Don't settle for a vision that you know you can achieve, but rather something that will require creative thought, discovery, and experimentation. Remember that your purpose here is to inspire and energize, not to tell people what to do.

At the same time, don't put the entire burden on yourself. As Kouzes and Posner point out, your job is not to be an emissary from the future with all the answers about what's next for your organization. Rather your job is to start the conversation, point the way, and ask provocative questions that can help everyone get excited and inspired about the future.

Step 3. Engage stakeholders

Once you come up with your own draft ideas, you need to engage others in developing and fleshing them out. Involving others with different perspectives ensures that you create the best vision possible and also jump-starts buy-in throughout the organization. For example, at the World Bank, Wolfensohn and his senior leaders actively engaged different stakeholders in providing input and iteratively co-creating the vision based on his initial commitment to poverty eradication. By involving others, he created a vision that tapped into everyone's passions, while also giving many people a voice in the process.

Every organization is different and every situation has its own unique characteristics and cast of characters, but to engage stakeholders, you first need to identify who to involve and then decide what the process of engagement will look like.

Who should you involve?

When choosing who to involve in the process, you'll need to consider who can provide valuable input and give you different perspectives, and who needs to buy in and be engaged in the process. Here are some questions to consider:

- **Do you want to limit the process to only a few people?** Should you include direct reports or team members or open it up to a wider group of employees, or even the whole department or organization? Working with a few senior people is faster, and you can facilitate debates directly, but you may disenfranchise many others. You also won't get as much input. On the other hand, when you engage more people, you also create expectations that you will consider their ideas, and they may be disappointed when their contributions don't make the cut. So you need to manage expectations carefully.

- **Do you want to engage your boss or other senior executives?** At some point, your boss will need to endorse your vision, since he or she is also accountable for the direction and aspirations for the larger department or enterprise. So the question is really not whether to engage your boss, but when. It's probably wise to alert your boss early on that you are rethinking or reshaping the vision, share your preliminary thoughts, and get his or her reactions and ideas. Then keep your boss abreast of the process and welcome input as you go along. By the time you present the vision to your senior executive and other senior people, they should already be on board. Similarly, if you are developing a vision for the enterprise, follow the same pattern, even up to and including the board.

- **Should you engage your customers?** Your customers and others outside the organization can provide a valuable point of view. Visions are usually much more robust if they have an outside-in flavor and reflect the perspective of the user, customer, or recipient of the organization's services, so we encourage you to bring your customers (internal or external) into the process. Take, for example, ConAgra Foods. When Gary Rodkin became the CEO in 2005, the firm was largely a holding company for prominent brands that it had acquired over the years (such as Hunt's, Orville Redenbacher, Hebrew National, Chef Boyardee, Marie Calendar, Butterball, and many others). As he stepped into the role, Rodkin talked extensively with its customers and realized that they really didn't view ConAgra as one company. Because it was dealing with each brand in a fragmented way, it was difficult for ConAgra to leverage its size in selling to large grocery retailers and outlets like Walmart. Rodkin's interactions with customers informed his vision to turn ConAgra into an $18 billion "integrated operating company" with a basket of brands that could negotiate with Walmart and others from a much stronger position.

As you consider the engagement of customers, however, remember that you may already have all the input you need from ongoing contacts and listening sessions, satisfaction surveys, and day-to-day relationships developed over time. If that's the case, getting more input from them might have diminishing returns. Toward the end of the process, however, you should share the emerging vision with some key customers to get their reactions, and use their feedback as a litmus test for whether you are on the right track.

What should the process be?

What's the process for engaging people, creating ownership, and coming up with a vision that meets the criteria we've discussed?

As with the types of people you involve, it's up to you to determine the right plan for your situation. There are some common approaches. One is to trigger the process with a rough first draft. Another is to provide a team with some key principles and then let team members sketch out a first draft (as Wolfensohn did at the World Bank). Another is to develop questions to address in focus groups or through interviews, and then use the emerging themes as a basis for the vision. As you decide on the right path, consider how you'll incorporate your point of view from the previous step into this process. Do you want to insist on it (as a principle)? Do you want it to be a starting point for conversation (as a first draft)?

For example, when Wesleyan University was revisiting its vision, its president Michael Roth began by writing a draft vision with a few colleagues. But Wesleyan had many different constituencies (faculty from many disciplines, alumni, students, employees, community) who all saw things from their own perspectives, so he knew it would be intensely criticized by other stakeholders, and it was. As Roth described, the vision needed to capture "the tension between being outlandish and Avant Garde; with wanting to be effective and making serious contributions; and between inclusivity and generosity of spirit through an education steeped in liberal arts. We wanted it to be broad enough for both a chemist and a musicologist." But as it circulated and his team changed it in response to the feedback, he saw it improving. Roth credits this process of passionate dialogue with the ultimate breadth of the vision.

That dialogue also needed to end. As he felt the team was getting close—that the vision was good enough—he announced that after ten more days, he would stop the process. The vision that Roth and Wesleyan ended up with was:

> To provide an education in the liberal arts that is characterized
> by boldness, rigor, and practical idealism . . . where distinguished
> scholar-teachers work closely with students, taking advantage of
> fluidity among disciplines to explore the world with a variety of
> tools . . . while building a diverse, energetic community of students,
> faculty, and staff who think critically and creatively and who
> value independence of mind and generosity of spirit.

From Roth's perspective, further debate would have added very little, made the statement overly complex, and not significantly improved the aspirational and exciting view of where the school was going.

Sometimes, of course, the approach to collaboration on a new vision is much less deliberate than this. Richard Ober, who is now CEO of the New Hampshire Charitable Foundation, was attending a conference earlier in his career when he was running a small but growing nonprofit. He had an epiphany about ideas that might be useful for a fund-raising brochure, so he drew a quick sketch of his ideas on a scrap of paper and then pulled it out a few days later at a development committee meeting. One of the board members said, "Hey, this isn't just a brochure—it's a vision for the whole organization," and the rest of the committee agreed. Only then did Ober bring the brochure to others in the organization to flesh it out. He presented it at an all-staff meeting where he took suggestions for what had been left out and then asked those who had participated to draft a more complete version. Those people began to develop ownership of the vision as a result.

Involving others in the vision process can be challenging for a leader, particularly if you already have a strong view of where you want your organization or team to go. This kind of debate requires that leaders accept that they are not the font of all wisdom and, in fact, may not have the best answer—a lesson in humility. It requires that you listen more than you broadcast. But this act isn't passive; it requires that you be highly engaged as you probe, ask questions, spot and challenge assumptions, and learn about different ways to frame the situation from many different people. It also requires you to actively synthesize many different ideas and viewpoints, and capture them in new, compelling ways. However deeply your own perspective is captured in the ultimate product, the process requires your creativity and energy for constant learning, pattern recognition, and effective articulation.

Step 4. Align people's work with the vision

Once you've finalized the vision statement itself, it's easy to think that you're done, especially if you've already involved a significant number of people in your organization or team in the process. The reality, however, is that engaging your people in creating or reshaping a vision is just the beginning. The next and perhaps most crucial step is to make the vision come alive by helping everyone on your team or in your organization see how their own work relates to it.

Many leaders assume that if they lead some high-level presentations and town meetings, hang some posters, and disseminate some videos, their people will understand the firm's vision and how their work contributes to it. While these are necessary vehicles for an intellectual understanding of where the organization is headed, they don't particularly help staff align the vision with their day-to-day work or help them tap its emotional potential.

Make it a conversation

As part of your campaign to share the vision throughout your department or organization, insist that managers at all levels bring their people together to actively work through the connections. They should lead these conversations not just once as you disseminate the new vision, or even just yearly during the annual planning cycle, but at regular intervals so that staff can incorporate new projects, initiatives, and issues into the overall direction and the aspirational and emotional fabric.

You should lead some of these conversations yourself, but you should also encourage other leaders and managers in your unit to do the same with their people. In these sessions, ask everyone to think about how they can connect the dots between the work they're doing and the vision of the company. What are the threads that tie together past initiatives and strategic directions with this vision? How have past efforts helped the company build capability over time and move toward the vision? What gets them excited about the vision? And if some of their projects or activities don't connect to the vision, should they be changed or discontinued?

Tell a story

A key skill as you sell a vision is the ability to tell a good story about it. Some business schools even include storytelling as part of their core curriculum. A story can connect the company's vision to real people, real situations, and real emotions so that people feel that their work makes a difference.

At the World Bank, for example, Wolfensohn and his team made the vision of poverty elimination come alive by describing particular projects and villages where the Bank was making a difference in real people's lives. Regional and country leaders at the Bank then did the same with their people. At ConAgra, Rodkin explained the vision of becoming an integrated operating company by telling stories about how real people in the company were working together across product areas and leveraging procurement scale to get better results.

At Xerox, Anne Mulcahy took the storytelling approach quite deliberately during her turnaround of the company in the late 1990s. In the midst of an intensive effort to save the company from bankruptcy, Mulcahy realized that her people were yearning for a higher level of purpose beyond day-to-day problem solving and operations. So she worked with one of her team members to write a fictional *Wall Street Journal* story, set several years in the future, that described how Xerox had pulled itself out of the crisis and made itself successful. Mulcahy hoped she could create "a story that people would see themselves in and be able to say, 'OK, I want to be part of that.'" It worked so well that for years afterward, she had to keep reminding people that the piece was fictional.

Another way to tell a story is to visualize it. A tool called a "from-to chart" can help capture the idea of where you are now versus where you are going to emphasize the direction that you are setting. (Table 1-5 shows an example of a from-to chart from Rodkin's vision at ConAgra.)

Unless you take the time to help your people understand the ways that the vision connects to their work and to their personal values and emotions, they may experience your new vision as a slogan on the wall or as one more change in a series of random and arbitrary directives with no rhyme or reason. By putting the vision into the context of employees' own experience, you'll have more success actually moving people in the direction that you've set—and making the vision into the best strategic unifier and motivator that it can be for your whole organization or team.

TABLE 1-5

From-to chart of ConAgra's vision

From	To
Brands selling independently	Brands selling together
Careers within one business unit or function	Careers across the company
Multiple supply chains	One supply chain
Dozens of different compensation plans	A limited compensation structure
Top-down command and control	Accountability for aligned objectives
A personnel department	HR focused on talent management

Questions to Consider

- **Vision alignment.** Does your team have a clear, shared vision for where it is going? If so, does it align with your personal vision for the team and the larger company vision?

- **Timing.** Is it time to revise or recraft the vision for your team? What would be the purpose of working on the vision now? How would it make a difference?

- **Future focus.** To what extent does your team's vision give everyone an exciting aspiration for the future? Does the vision look far enough ahead to get everyone thinking creatively about their work?

- **Being bold.** What big ideas do you have about your team's vision? Can you paint a picture of the future that people would be excited about working toward—and that would engage their hearts as well as their heads?

- **Stakeholders.** Who do you need to involve in crafting or modifying your team's vision? Team members? Internal or external customers? Your boss? Other stakeholders?

- **Process.** What process will you use to craft or modify your team's vision? Will you take a first cut? Can you assign the work to a team? Should you bring everyone together? Can you use virtual conversations or your internal social media?

- ■ **Communication.** What stories can you use to bring your vision to life so it's not just a slogan or catchphrase? Can you portray the vision with a from-to chart?

2.

Developing a Strategy

The essence of strategy is making choices . . . One of the leader's jobs is to teach others in the organization about strategy—and also to say no.

—Michael Porter

In chapter 1, we introduced "vision"—the practice of creating a unifying picture of success for the future. To realize a vision, you need a strategy—a coordinated set of concrete actions to reach the vision and achieve impact in the market. Welcome to our second leadership practice.

Many strategy discussions are faddish (e.g., one-size-fits-all solutions for greatness) or misleading (e.g., in the fast-moving global economy, strategy is dead). But strategy always depends on a company's particular situation, and though it has evolved far beyond corporate planning, the concept is hardly dead.

Developing strategic thinking and learning to assess the trade-offs of different strategic choices will help you grow as a leader. Several executives that we interviewed highlighted how successful strategies boosted both the impact of the organization and their own leadership, too: CEO David Winn's breakthrough retail strategy for American Express France in the 1990s earned him a subsequent stream of top job career opportunities; General Stanley McChrystal was celebrated for the daring network strategy that dramatically degraded Al Qaeda during the Iraq War; Anne Mulcahy became one of the most influential CEOs of her day for her strategy that rescued Xerox from bankruptcy.

But strategy is not just for CEOs. Most organizations have an overall corporate strategy that is supported by smaller, more focused strategies for specific business units to roll out individual products or services or to guide specific initiatives. Strategy making at any level offers rich opportunities for you to hone your leadership skills—by analyzing your unit's situation, understanding different choices for operating within your market, and building commitment among other people for a particular course of action. Throughout the process, you also can learn why, when, and how to stick to those decisions—saying no to initiatives that take your intended strategy off track.

We'll show you the enduring fundamentals of this practice and then walk you through six steps of strategy making—from defining a process, to making decisions and implementing them—so that you can increase your own leadership impact.

We'll begin with a recent case of a strategy-making process within a relatively large organization: how a small team of unit leaders at the Public Broadcasting Service (PBS) developed, through cycles of adaptive learning, a strategy for a new 24/7 children's educational TV channel. The strategy—which resulted in one of the most successful service launches in recent PBS history—began as a bottom-up initiative and had to overcome the initial doubts of PBS's CEO.

A strategy for a dedicated children's channel at PBS

Children's programming has long been part of PBS's cultural and educational mission. But beloved shows such as *Sesame Street* and *Daniel Tiger's*

Neighborhood have historically had to compete for airtime with all the other programming that local member stations distribute, so the hours of children's educational broadcasting are always limited.

In 2005 PBS made a strategic move to reach more children beyond its member stations' segmented schedules: it joined a consortium of partners to launch an additional nationwide channel dedicated solely to kids' programming (at launch, the channel was called PBS Kids Sprout) that would be distributed, through cable and satellite, throughout the day and evening. The channel was initially successful, but in 2013, because of some of the partners' shifting priorities and other educational concerns, PBS (under the direction of CEO Paula Kerger) chose to withdraw from the partnership.

Following the withdrawal, Lesli Rotenberg, PBS's senior vice president and general manager of children's media and education, continued to see an opportunity for PBS to expand its educational service to children. As she talked to local station managers and looked at Nielsen ratings and other data such as Google Analytics to better understand children's viewing patterns, she saw that there was a continuing need for more quality children's programming, especially during weekday evenings and throughout all hours of the weekend. She also believed if PBS now built its own kids' service, separate from its onetime partners, it not only would expand overall preschool audiences, but could help realize a vision Kerger had been emphasizing—reaching more children in TV households that couldn't afford cable channels or access to broadband internet. Rotenberg pitched Kerger on building a new, all-PBS children's channel.

Her boss was skeptical at first. "I didn't think there was a big enough market for us alone, nor that local stations had spectrum available for a dedicated channel," Kerger recalled. "I told Lesli she'd have to convince me with some real numbers, and a viable new strategy."

As Rotenberg gathered data and built a business case, Kerger met with her periodically to review her findings, always remaining tough on her general manager. From the start, Kerger insisted that the new strategy answer three questions: Is there a market need and opportunity for PBS to do this alone? Are local stations willing and able to deliver it? Can PBS organizationally develop and sustain it at current investment levels?

"This concept has to be both market-driven and sustainable. We can't fritter away resources on a one-shot idea," Kerger told Rotenberg. But upon reflection, the PBS CEO began to see some broader potential: "Media landscapes were changing because of digital—and this was particularly true for children's media. I urged Lesli to team up with Ira Rubenstein, head of our digital group, and to collaborate on shaping a strategy."

Working together, Rotenberg and Rubenstein began to see the benefits of choosing a more multiplatform approach. Their excitement grew as team members brainstormed ways to integrate educational games with television programming, based on research that proved children's learning accelerates when they play games and video connected to the same curriculum goals. They started to pull in other PBS functions, too (technology, member relations, etc.), including Renard Jenkins of engineering, to expand their innovative thinking and to make the operational details more concrete.

As this expanded team marshaled more specifics for a new children's channel, Kerger became its coach. The CEO kept the pressure on, but also reinforced the team's collaborative problem-solving approach, helping members learn from each other's expertise. In this way, they tackled technical problems like extending the reach of regular broadcast programming, while also developing pedagogical ideas at the intersection of digital and broadcast. They also brainstormed different ways to minimize costs. When Kerger set a goal for the number of PBS stations that had to commit to the new service for it to be sustainable, the strategy team began to regularly engage local leaders. Those discussions helped the team shape the outlines of the new programming service, while also assessing implications for building and maintaining the channel.

Through research and ongoing discussions with member stations, the strategy team members developed options for answering Kerger's initial questions. They then worked to narrow those down to their final answers, which resulted in the following:

- There was indeed a quantifiable market opportunity in communities for a new 24/7 PBS KIDS channel offering the organization's historically high-quality programming, especially with the decision to target higher engagement among children, including more lower-income households (via broadcast) and a growing population attracted to online streaming (via digital).

- There were also opportunities to expand PBS's reach to certain community institutions (such as hospitals, where children were up at odd hours watching television).

- Member stations had spectrum available that they would use to broadcast this programming around the clock to their communities, and a significant number were prepared to make a commitment to do so.

- A new 24/7 children's service could be financially viable if it could build on existing shows and add digital features incrementally, and if PBS units outside the kids' team would prioritize this project over other initiatives. With this approach, existing budgets could therefore support the service, as operating units shared both new development and ongoing operational tasks by working together more closely.

These recommendations represented some tough choices for PBS and the team. The success of the initiative would depend on the participation of a sufficient number of member stations and on PBS's willingness to redirect people resources. It would also require PBS to commit to a project that would have a permanent impact on the organization's operating budget.

The team's can-do approach, however, encouraged cost-saving collaboration and helped smooth over what might have otherwise been turf battles. Instead of competing for budgets, the members shared resources to reduce duplication of effort and hiring. The children's unit cut back development of brand-new content, instead relying on existing educational programming. The digital team focused its efforts on bringing the channel online via a livestream feed. And engineering prioritized its technical work to accommodate the new service. Kerger explained some of the choices they made as part of the strategy process: "We traded off developing some near-term new programming to build a stronger, longer-term growth platform through which even more programming will be delivered in coming years."

Once Kerger embraced the team's strategy proposal, she began to advocate for the service across the network. In the latter half of 2016, when enough member stations signaled their formal interest and commitments on both sides were agreed, the CEO green-lighted the project for launch. The PBS KIDS 24/7 channel (as it was now branded) was formally rolled out in January 2017.

The CEO and the strategy team, working together and with member stations, had created a unique offering: the only 24/7 nationally distributed channel of engaging, curriculum-based, noncommercial educational programming, available for free, enhanced with links to educational digital games, available on children's digital devices at home or for viewing wherever they might be. Engaging, multiplatform, interactive, and pedagogically rigorous, PBS KIDS 24/7 was like nothing else in the market. And it was successful: a large majority of the stations committed to PBS KIDS 24/7 in the first year, making it available to 95 percent of all US TV households. It was a big step forward in recognizing Kerger's vision and the mission of the organization: PBS ratings among kids increased by 23 percent—including growth of 85 percent among children in low-income families.

Kerger views the strategy for the offering's development and launch as one of the more successful in her tenure at the network. She is quick to give credit to Lesli Rotenberg and the full team that created it together. (Kerger today recalls her pride and wonder at seeing how many different contributors to the effort were in the room at the party celebrating the channel launch.) PBS KIDS 24/7 went on to become a valuable piece of the broader PBS corporate strategy in place at the time, focused on developing quality noncommercial content and strong distribution, strengthening the health of the PBS member station network, and building a culture of innovation.

What is a strategy?

We define strategy as a coordinated set of actions that organizations, divisions, and teams follow to win: to create distinctive value for customers, differentiate their performance, beat out competitors, and move toward the vision they've set. Leaders develop a strategy by guiding their people through choices about *where* and *how* to compete for customers that are better than their rivals'. (Our perspective here is indebted to seminal works by Peter Drucker, A. G. Lafley, Roger Martin, and Michael Porter.)

Following a coordinated set of intentional actions is a reminder that strategy is not accidental. Though companies and initiatives occasionally thrive by being in the right place at the right time, enduring business success requires that the group's actions be deliberate. PBS KIDS 24/7 didn't simply fall into its new strategy; it was coordinated by Rotenberg and the full team under Kerger's leadership.

The phrase "where and how to compete" points to the kinds of options and decisions you'll sift through to develop strategic choices for your unit or initiative. In creating products, services, or other business programs, you'll have to decide about particular arenas to focus on (e.g., customers in a certain geography, industry, or market space) and the way you'll serve your chosen customers (e.g., by offering some combination of benefits, pricing, branding, additional support, etc.). For example, for their new initiative at PBS, Rotenberg and the team chose to develop an offering for broadcast *and* digital, and they also decided not to partner with other outlets, as they had with Sprout.

The idea of choices is critical here, because, as Michael Porter famously said, "Strategy is as much about what you decide *not* to do, as what you *do* do." The mark of a failing strategy is trying to be all things to all people— and not having the courage of focus. The best strategies develop offerings targeting some unique and defensible sweet spot—a winning blend among multiple variables, for example, satisfying the needs of certain customers; doing that with the right combination of product or service attributes at the right cost; shaping the offerings on the basis of particular strengths of your team; and doing it all in a way that makes it hard for competitors to beat you at the same game. Find the right strategic sweet spot and you can win too.

The process of strategy

Of course, strategies sometimes fail (even spectacularly, as famous case studies will attest). Your growth as a leader must be built not just on successes but also on learning from your setbacks. Strategy making will provide plenty of those, too, along the way. Don't shrink from the challenges.

But as a rising leader, you should also understand why strategies fail. Two common pitfalls are:

- Incorrectly assessing an external market situation or misjudging an internal capability needed for the strategy—or both

- Being surprised by a trend that suddenly changes the game of your business—for example, a new technology or unforeseen competitor that arises

In today's dynamic global economy, such risks are increasingly common. You should do your best to minimize those risks, but even the savviest strategists can still get caught off guard.

The practice of strategy is changing as leaders more deliberately attempt to hedge against failure and adapt more nimbly to changing circumstances. The lengthy, internally focused planning processes of yore have given way to much more flexible, outward-facing, short-cycle, and learn-as-one-goes-along approaches—reflecting the mindset and so-called lean methods seen in many Silicon Valley startups. (This kind of thinking was epitomized in Steve Blank's HBR article "Why the Lean Start-Up Changes Everything," but the concepts were introduced earlier in Rita Gunther McGrath and Ian Macmillan's 1995 HBR article "Discovery-Driven Planning.") A lean approach may seem more informal and practical, but it is not without its own structure and logic. Great leaders still follow a deliberate and structured problem-solving process to identify critical choices and develop decisions to shape their strategies. And so should you.

So what are the essential steps? What is the best way to find the right balance, on the one hand, between analysis and deliberation to make the right choices, and on the other, embracing speed, flexibility, and openness to adaptation, suited to today's faster and more unpredictable climate?

Developing a process to make your strategic choices

You don't frame and make such strategic choices in a vacuum. You identify and shape them through a deliberate problem-solving process, working with others, over time. Even if strategy making now happens faster, more informally, and more flexibly than previous planning-intensive approaches, some methodological discipline will sharpen your thinking and structure your learning. Let's walk through some typical problem-solving steps to help you develop the right choices of a winning strategy.

Step 1. Set the stage

First, be clear what you're generally trying to accomplish with your strategy making and how you want to go about it. Start with a simple checklist of key questions and tasks to guide your journey.

- **Purpose.** Why generally are you developing a new strategy? What's driving the need or opportunity to do that? Do you need a fresh approach to achieving your vision, or do you have a new vision? Your strategy should begin by answering a simple powerful question about the intent of your effort.

  At PBS, Kerger helped focus Rotenberg's desire to expand the children's market with a new kids' channel by asking if there was a need for that and, if so, could the network viably do it on its own?

- **Audience and stakeholders.** Who will the strategy potentially benefit, who must be involved in developing it, and who must ultimately approve it? Key stakeholders might be, for example, major influencers in the organization, board members, or frontline people who would have to be centrally involved in delivering the strategy. It might also, later if not sooner, include customers, partners, and other relevant players in the external environment. (You'll have to balance the risk of potential competitors being alerted to your ideas through such external discussions with the benefit of gaining valuable input.)

At PBS, Kerger coached Rotenberg that the strategy, though ultimately aimed at children and parent viewers, would have to be built by—and ultimately be embraced by—both the broader organization of PBS and the leaders of the network's local stations.

- **Scope, constraints, and potential implementation implications.** What arenas and unit of analysis must the strategy be situated within? (That is, is the strategy for a particular business unit, initiative, or a broader part of the enterprise?) Are there limits or boundaries to what can be pursued from the outset? If the strategy is accepted, what ripple effects will follow? What are the implications for other corporate units? Customers? Brand identity? And so on.

  At PBS, the new channel began as a service strategy within the children's educational unit, but as it evolved, it touched most other parts of the organization. From the start, it was always seen as supporting the broader vision of the network. At the same time, Kerger imposed important constraints on the level of investment that would be available for the new service.

- **Participants, engagement, deliverables.** What kind of team will work to create the strategy? How will its members work with one another and the broader universe of stakeholders? Will there be off-sites, virtual meetings, multiple strategic planning sessions? How many, when, and so on? And what final form will the strategy take?

The creation of any strategy demands finding the right balance between involving key stakeholders and experts in the problem solving but also keeping the effort small enough to remain nimble and practical. The best projects, as the PBS team represented, are a hybrid: organized as a

Don't go it alone

Whatever your role (and relative authority), you should not assume that the strategy-making process rests only on your shoulders. You will have to approve what the strategy on your watch will be, but it's important that you understand the constraints and opportunities under which you are operating and who else will have a share in the overall accountability. If you are asked to develop a strategy for your unit's contribution to broader company strategy, you will likely receive a set of assumptions and resources that will bound the options you'll be able to develop.

But whatever the scope of your ultimate strategy-making responsibility, resist the temptation to be the all-seeing, heroic decision maker. You'll develop better options by listening to other people along the way—calling on other professionals, working collaboratively across and beyond the organization—to ensure that your process is identifying the right problem areas and exploring the most viable ideas. It's also valuable to get help and outside perspective on analyzing and modeling the financial and implementation considerations of different ideas. Fresh eyes can minimize what is often inevitable confirmation bias.

Great leaders we've spoken with stress the importance of letting go and being open to perspectives other than their own as they consider strategy solutions. Kerger readily admits today she was too skeptical when Rotenberg approached her about the new dedicated kids' channel. It is to her credit that, even as she challenged her general manager, she kept an open mind about an initiative she had doubts about.

Trying to minimize your own personal prejudices is especially important when hearing objections and concerns about your ideas. The best leaders make a conscious effort to listen to others, and to know and restrain their own biases. Being able to hear dissent means that you'll "understand why the status quo doesn't have to be the way business is done," in the wise words of Tamara Lundgren, CEO of Schnitzer Steel.

(continued)

Furthermore, failing to take into account the viewpoints of others in your organization or immediate team means you'll be taking all that work on yourself—and usually not for the better. As Charlie Brown, founder of the community design firm Context Partners, told us: "When I first started my company, I felt the CEO job was to provide all the answers. I kept floundering until some employees and clients finally told me: '[Your company] will do much better if you stop trying to do it all yourself. The strategy needs to leverage a wider network of other people.' I've now made that the rule for how we operate."

small central team that then involves other contributors periodically as needed. The team ultimately led by Rotenberg and Rubenstein was a core of children's media and technical experts from different PBS units, but its members regularly met and shaped the project with input from other leaders and key staff from member stations across the system. (See the box "Don't go it alone.")

As your team starts to work, identify the final products your effort must produce and for whom: Will it be a written plan, a presentation for your boss, or an executive-style memo for your CEO? Will it include (as such things normally do) specific goals and objectives, a fit with a vision, analyses, a rationale for the initiative, a financial model, competitive analyses, an assessment of risks and rewards, and so on?

Give some initial thought to how you will communicate the final strategy and extend it to the broader organization. Involving as many stakeholders as possible in the process—including frontline employees—will smooth the way for greater acceptance. For those not actively involved, good communication will be particularly necessary. At PBS, Kerger noted that a major success of the PBS KIDS 24/7 strategy was how broadly and continuously the team had built participation and enthusiasm across multiple units of the organization.

Step 2. Set strategic goals

After such preliminaries, talk to your team about what success for the strategy making overall might look like—how to imagine what a great result would be. To get more concrete, think next about some specific goals and how the strategy will help move your organization toward whatever kind of future vision might be in place (see the box "Check in on your vision").

Because lean-style strategy making involves iterative learning and evolution of thinking, different strategic choices will likely emerge through your process, but whatever the path forward, the final measures of success (what you're ultimately aiming to achieve) will likely stay pretty constant. Choose measures that clearly signify value and impact consistent with your team's vision and the broader vision of your company. The goals you choose should resonate with your key stakeholders, too.

In the PBS KIDS case, Kerger and the strategy team agreed early on that the programming for the potential new channel would have to reach a particular audience size, measured by a threshold of member affiliates that would agree to carry the service; and they placed special emphasis on reaching more lower-income households. They also understood that the channel and its programming would have to be in line with the PBS mission of educational improvement of the nation and the network's corporate strategy of building and distributing quality content, ensuring strong member stations, and promoting innovation.

Different businesses and different strategies will have different measures of success. A business unit with a vision of, say, reaching a new level of market growth might set strategic goals that are top-line financial targets for specific customer segments or achieving a percentage of revenue derived from new products. For a civic or governmental organization committed to, say, eliminating poverty, strategic goals might be providing a level of food and shelter security for a specific community or increasing its level of employment. For David Winn, who became CEO of the failing American Express Bank in France, the organizational vision was to revitalize the institution with the consumer financial expertise of the global corporation; he set strategic goals to make the bank profitable again and expand market share against financial competitors. General Stanley Mc-Chrystal's mission when he took over the Joint Special Operations Command in Iraq was to slow the terrorism of Al Qaeda; he was working toward a vision of establishing a more peaceful Iraq and Afghanistan that wouldn't harbor terrorists. The strategic goal he set was to kill or capture as many Al Qaeda leaders as possible.

A good strategy should aspire to achieve a limited number of relevant goals that stakeholders of the organization can easily understand; it should

Check in on your vision

Because great strategy flows from vision, early on you'll need to check in on your team's and your organization's bigger pictures of success. This is where the vision practice comes into play. If your team doesn't have a clear aspiration to rally around, you can't do the strategy work to reach that kind of success: if you're not clear about your destination, how can you choose any particular approach to get there? Clarity about your destination should also enable you to think more wisely about the different routes you ought to consider.

You must also ask yourself about your deeper motivation: is the desire for a new strategy really a desire for a new vision, too? Be honest. Sometimes, a team's vision does need refreshing or altering; that may become clear only as you start to develop a new strategy.

Because vision and strategy are so closely related—"where we want to get to, how we will do it"—they often evolve in tandem. If you feel you have to develop (or newly develop) a vision together with strategy, don't let the dual process become an endless loop or have your strategy force a larger change of purpose than the organization really needs. In the end, vision should be broad and durable enough to benefit from different strategies in different situations. As markets, technology, and competitive situations change, you may well need to develop new strategies to achieve the same picture of success embodied in your vision.

also simply explain how achieving them will reflect progress toward its vision. (Goals are usually further broken down into specific objectives and intermediate outcomes for executional planning; see chapter 4.)

Step 3. Understand your current situation

Once you've set goals tied to your unit's or your company's larger vision and strategy, turn your team toward understanding the status quo. Make an honest appraisal of your team's existing business—current performance, assets, capabilities, basis for competition, and so on. Then do the same for the world in which your unit and broader company operates, looking at how that landscape is changing (e.g., shifting consumer tastes, new competitors emerging, new technology restructuring business models, etc.) and the threats and opportunities that come with those changes. This dual assessment will provide the starting point for developing ideas and opportunities to improve or even transform where and how you compete and deciding on a distinctive value proposition.

You can approach the appraisal of your existing team in many ways. It may vary depending on how well the performance of your company is already documented and understood, and the level of analytical rigor you feel is now needed. A radically lean effort might begin with minimal analysis or a starter sketch that is then iteratively tested and refined, but a few fundamental questions must nonetheless be addressed, for example, "Who are we today and how does that fit with the external world and new challenges?"

Other frameworks can help with such questions. Consider, for example, Peter Drucker's theory of the business—the often tacit assumptions of "policies, practices, and behaviors" about how (and how well) your company operates and how well those fit today's competitive climate. Or you may want to analyze your business model in more detail, which includes your key value proposition to customers; how you make money (which is important whether you are for-profit or nonprofit); and the processes and resources you rely on to deliver value. The current situation appraisal should also consider aspects of talent, financial and technology resources, culture, brand, and similar assets to bring to your strategy for winning.

The second part of the task—understanding the external world in which you operate—is complex: you must consider not just existing markets, customers, and competitors, but also those emerging and changing due to social, economic, and technological trends. This is also the time to assess major discontinuities in markets and how emerging new players are reinventing ways to serve the traditional needs of customers (including what Clayton Christensen has famously labeled *disruption*) or creating whole new markets that previously didn't exist.

Frontline workers are important sources for getting these perspectives (another reason for including people with pivotal jobs in your strategic task force). In all cases, you should be sure to tap their experience and observations—both about forces at work externally (changing customer needs, new competitors arising, pricing pressure, etc.) and internally (e.g., organizational obstacles or operational inefficiencies blocking your company's ability to compete).

Many off-the-shelf analyses assess internal and external issues, and armies of consultants are happy to help you further, often with their own special tools, including an increasing set of analytical and big data interpretative technologies. But beware: you can be easily overwhelmed by the amount of analysis you may think you have to do, even (and, sometimes, especially) when you have consultant help. (See the box "When to bring in consultants.") Constraints and the pace of competition will here again force you to make some choices. Constantly ask yourself whether the ongoing investigation is still adding substantial benefit to the process. Keep building your experience about the kind of effort needed: ideally, when you've done enough to get the picture roughly right, but not so much that momentum and opportunity are lost due to analysis paralysis. These are judgment calls that distinguish effective from less effective leaders.

In the PBS case, Kerger challenged Rotenberg not only to explore the market need and station capacity for a stand-alone children's channel, but also to leverage the knowledge of Rubenstein and his colleagues in the digital unit about technology's evolving impact on the media landscape. That could have expanded into an almost endless research project, but by working with a few established experts, mining PBS's already rich audi-

When to bring in consultants

Strategy consultants can be helpful, but it's a mistake to hand over all the thinking about your strategy to outsiders. You and your team may not have the capacity to run a strategy project alone, but you will need to be centrally involved and own the process. Consultants can minimize the burden by providing facilitation and specialized expertise. Consultants can also be helpful in holding up a mirror to your organization and framing questions objectively, without political bias. But the final strategy must belong to you and your organization, not the outsiders.

ence research, and also filtering what was being learned with the judgment of various local station managers, the PBS strategy team found the right balance to be sufficiently comprehensive—but not needlessly exhaustive—to make the design choices required for a new channel.

Identify key issues and problems to solve

In synthesizing your findings from the internal and external investigations, strive to identify the key issues and problems to solve, that is, where there's a mismatch or clear opportunity arising when you compare trends or external conditions and what your organization is currently doing. Your central task is to select questions relevant to the strategy that will frame key choices and ultimately shape the overall strategy.

For example, as the research unfolded, the PBS team realized the strategy for the new children's channel would have to address several critical issues: specifically designing the programming service for the channel to deepen engagement and learning opportunities with the target audience of children in low-income households; identifying the most promising opportunities for integrating broadcast content with digital games; differentiating the new channel from others in the children's media marketplace; determining the operational implications of the cross-platform approach; uncovering the financial and technical implications of adding a new channel to the operations of current member stations; and many others.

Step 4. Develop options for where and how to compete

Once you're clear on your goals and understand your team's current situation (both internally and externally), you can begin to identify the key choices defining your strategy. The shorthand we've been using for strategy making—"deciding where and how to compete"—reflects the two core, interrelated decisions that represent your formula for making an impact in pursuit of your vision. They will ultimately frame the kind of sweet spot of unique and defensible value your strategy must strive to create.

Remember, as discussed in our original definition, "where" and "how" to compete are placeholders for several more subtle themes. "Where" might be literally geographical—a particular market in France or a specific theater of operations in Iraq. But it can also signify a certain group of customers, defined by selected demographic characteristics, or a group of companies in an industry sector, or making a division between wholesale and retail channels, or many other things. (Because segmentation of market opportunity has become its own rarefied science, you may need some specialized expertise to help.)

How to compete can refer to a product or a service, the particular markets through which you sell them, or some combination of both. "How" can also refer to the specific approach you choose for your packaging, pricing, branding, financing, customer service, and many other things, including whether you do these things in-house, purchase them from outside, or acquire new capabilities (see the box "Exploring make-or-buy and acquisition options"). "How" combines the "what," "why," and "in what manner" that you are using to create distinctive value for your "who." In McChrystal's military case, the how–to-compete issue turned on building a new culture of information sharing among disparate military and civilian units, so they would collaborate better and faster to strike terrorists across the Middle East. For Winn's American Express bank, it was the design—features, pricing, regulatory compliance, check-writing services, interest-paying

Exploring make-or-buy and acquisition options

A potential choice in the process is whether to make or buy the new products, services, or other sources of revenue on which the strategy will depend. Leaders will often look outside to do an acquisition or to develop a solution they think will be more cost-effective, faster, or more innovative than what they can develop in their own company.

Acquiring another entity, whatever the reason, can be a large and fraught undertaking, and if you are not a CEO, it's not likely something you'd pursue without a lot of support from more senior leaders. That said, if you still think such a move has value for your strategy, understand a few implications before you get started.

First, know that the shorthand phrase—"make versus buy"—sets up what might be a false binary choice. There is always a spectrum of other corporate options for developing new skills or assets to consider, including contracting for new services, forging product or market-specific partnerships, forming more extensive joint ventures, and the like (for more, see Laurence Capron and Will Mitchell's book *Build, Borrow, or Buy*).

Second, make sure you've also really given the internal option a fair shake. You may have too quickly assumed that the knowledge, skills, or assets needed for your strategy don't exist in your company. Sometimes the resources required do exist internally, but they're not in your specific part of the organization, or they're not currently accessible because of how your company is structured. You can create new efficiencies or spark corporate innovation when separate units start collaborating across boundaries (as in the PBS case with the children's media and digital units). If you're developing new strategies for your unit, consider if you have colleagues elsewhere in the company with whom you can partner to achieve what's needed and that could benefit both of your units.

(continued)

If a full-blown external acquisition is indeed the best answer for your new strategy, reach out early for the appropriate advice and support you need from your own leadership and relevant external experts. You can get ready for those discussions with some additional preparation:

1. Consider how a potential acquisition would directly enhance your specific strategy. Remember that acquisitions are only a tool to support a strategy, not a strategy itself. Know also that different kinds of strategies will be served by different kinds of acquisitions (e.g., depending on whether you are doing product extensions versus whole-scale reinvention of your business model; see the HBR article "The New M&A Playbook," by Clayton Christensen et al.).

2. Face the fact that acquisitions are almost always more complicated and uncertain than they might seem at first; research shows that some 70 percent fail or fall short of expectations. Are you ready to handle the potential financial and reputational risk you and your company may be taking on if you move ahead?

3. Take advantage of some advance what-if scenario analysis to understand how viable your potential acquisition can really be. Ron has laid out a framework for smart "backward planning" in his HBR article "Are You Really Ready for an Acquisition?" He suggests creating a high-level picture of what the combined company or merger would look like after a year of integration (financing but also organizational structure, processes, culture, staffing, etc.) and then back-solving what it would take to get there, including resources and time (investment, teams, processes), governance and oversight, essential skills, and so on.

rates, and so on—of a new retail product at the heart of a transformed consumer strategy.

The PBS children's channel focused on a strategy of "where" that would target children and parents (especially mothers) in member station communities and also particularly try to reach both children in lower-income households without cable access and others using digital devices for streaming. The "how" of the strategy that eventually emerged was to develop a high-quality, curriculum-based, noncommercial educational service that was cross-platform in delivery and interactivity.

From problems to opportunities

To begin developing the "where" and "how" choices for your strategy, consider the problems you identified in the previous step—for example, an out-of-date business model, encroaching competitors, maturing product lines, and so on. As you consider these problems, your analysis may well suggest new ideas to do something excitingly better and different. Look for opportunities for winning in some new way, suited to the changing environment, such as leveraging a new technology to improve your cost position, redeploying your talent to improve a customer experience, or adapting products to changing cultural tastes. You may also want to consider whether partnering or even acquiring another business may open new opportunities for creating more value for customers. Keep asking yourself and your strategy team: Is there something superior and distinctive we could do, in light of what we're learning about our company and its competitive, external operating context?

Developing the best strategic options requires creativity in addition to analytic skills. Leaders can often boost creative capability by examining innovative approaches to growth in other businesses and brainstorming whether there are patterns that they could adapt to their own company. You can also find fresh thinking outside your strategy-making team: have the members brainstorm with your frontline people, explore new innovative approaches by collaborating with lead customers, or call on networks beyond your company. For example, you could partner with a university or design firm, or work with outside experts to adapt a wholly different business model from another industry.

Throughout our executive interviews, we constantly heard about strategy making that was based on options developed by learning from others—McKinsey's global managing partner Dominic Barton raising up innovative client service approaches that were being experimented with in different corners of the firm's global network; Tamara Lundgren applying new approaches to mortgage securitization in Europe based on technologies she had utilized in the United States to create more innovative products earlier in her career for Deutsche Bank; Stan McChrystal literally borrowing some of the network organization's playbook from his enemy to create the more nimble, information-sharing culture of Allied Special Operations in Iraq. At PBS, with Kerger coaching her, Rotenberg expanded her horizons by engaging other colleagues who, with her, developed the idea of a combined broadcast and digital service, with crossover content and interactive learning games linked to the broadcast programming.

Narrowing the possibilities

The PBS strategy team fleshed out its final strategic choices through more discussion and problem solving between the broadcast and digital units of the organization, and its ongoing research with member stations, too—allowing all stakeholders to learn from one another and understand the costs and benefits of a dedicated, multiplatform channel. The team was able to finalize decisions based on some fact-based projections of audience size and a lot of carefully collected and analyzed feedback from—and specific commitments made by—local stations in the network.

As you start to develop different options for your strategy—by exploring different combinations of where and how to compete—you'll need to identify certain filters for making your final bets. One set of filters should be Porter's five essential tests of a good strategy (see the box "Five tests for your strategy"). Beyond those, a few other usual suspects should also be part of your investigations: standard cost, benefit, risk considerations; the likelihood that your organization can deliver on the value proposition; how much flexibility you have to fall back on or change direction if the new strategy doesn't work out; whether a particular option will also provide learning to more generally improve future performance; and, of course, how well the strategy fits with your vision for the group, as well as the strategy and vision of your organization overall.

Five tests for your strategy

In her book *Understanding Michael Porter*, Joan Magretta distills Porter's principles of creating and sustaining competitive advantage down to five tests. You've seen how Kerger and Rotenberg and the team shaped their strategy around these kinds of elements; you can also use them to make your own key decisions. Every good strategy must have:

- **A distinctive value proposition.** The decisions you make about where and how to compete are trade-offs—within the context of your larger company, which customers will you choose to serve, and which of their needs, with which offerings, packaging, pricing, and so forth? How will these be better than and different from alternatives in the marketplace?

- **A tailored value chain.** It's one thing to come up with a unique offering for a selected target audience, but you also must deliver on it, especially in a way that would be difficult to replicate by competitors. This may mean changing how you work, restructuring your organization, or taking on (or cutting back on) additional costs.

- **Trade-offs that enable your differentiation from rivals.** As we've mentioned, strategy is as much about what you decide *not* to do, because without focusing your effort and resources, it will be difficult to reach a threshold of being distinctive in something. A lack of focus waters down the emphasis and energy you're trying to compete with against other players. Because no organization can be all things to all customers, and resources are never infinite, you'll have to stop doing some things. Choose the right ones.

(continued)

- **Strategic fit.** The concept of strategic fit is elusive but important—making sure the strategy is designed and tailored to do what your organization does better than others, accords with your culture and values, and calls on internal capabilities that are well aligned with the external needs you are serving. When the parts of your strategy fit together seamlessly and naturally, it works like a self-amplifying system, providing what some strategy experts have called "a coherence premium" (see Paul Leinwand and Cesare Manardi's HBR article "The Coherence Premium").

- **Continuity over time.** Though strategies inevitably require new thinking and new ways of working, changing too much or too quickly can undermine success, too. Innovation should not burn all bridges with your heritage, lest you confuse customers or undo the trust on which your future relationships will depend.

As you start to formulate different options, you'll feel the risks and pressure to make the right choices. Careful analysis and using the right filters will be critical, but bear in mind that going from "where we are" to "where we want to be" can't be achieved only by rational calculation. You can't analyze your way into some brilliant new way of operating, nor can you surely predict what new product or service is going to take off and help your organization soar. Improve your chances of success by also considering less tangible factors, for example, how urgent the need for a new strategy may be; whether the timing is right to make a big change or it's better to wait until later; how emotionally ready your team is to undertake a certain new strategy idea versus another; the potential ripple effects—both positive and negative—on the organization beyond your own unit or operating group; whether you have the talent on board to do what's needed, and if not, whether you can find and hire them quickly enough; and whether you yourself have enough confidence and strength to do what's needed. Which now brings us to you and your leadership role in getting to final decisions and action.

Step 5. Assess options, engage stakeholders, move toward decisions

As smart and hardworking as your strategy team may be, it won't get everything right the first time around, and you as the leader must set the tone for your people to learn and adapt toward the best possible answers. New information will appear, situations will change, bugs will surface that will reveal flaws in your "where" and "how" choices. Good strategy making, especially in today's operating climate, is more of an ongoing process than a decision that you make once and forever. The recognition of this reality is why lean approaches are growing in popularity, shifting away from more static strategy formulation and planning that presupposed completeness once key senior leaders had spoken.

That's not to say that developing strategy doesn't require some final decision making and, indeed, moving from analyzing and debating options to real action. Knowing when to make that critical shift is where good leadership makes a real difference. The boundary between such steps is more blurred now, and strategy is generally more iterative—marked by testing, learning, and continuous adjustment, not punctuated finality. In its own simple way, the PBS KIDS 24/7 story, with a solution that slowly evolved and improved over time, is one more example of the trend.

As you develop your own strategy, consider embracing at least two learn-by-doing aspects of the lean startup approach. First, as you identify different options of where and how to compete, try out the ideas with key stakeholders whom you identified earlier in the process and refine accordingly.

Second, consider taking a further step to test your ideas—literally run trials or experiments of your most promising options (e.g., building a prototype, mock-up, or simulation of your product or service, and then sharing it with stakeholders to observe usage, bugs, and operational challenges).

Such testing will reveal what works and what doesn't, and you'll doubtless gain insights to make your strategy even better. Testing can also break the paralysis of uncertainty, as Ron and Logan Chandler wrote in their HBR article "Four Tips for Better Strategic Planning." Finally, testing and experimentation can help you more deeply understand barriers to overcome and the resources and systems for implementation at scale. It could also highlight new aspects of value that you can package and sell, or add to your marketing campaign.

You can use testing for any strategy-making process, though your situation may call for different levels of rigor. Common practices include setting up specific hypotheses to test, comparison between control groups and groups experiencing the new product or service, iterative refinement of the offering based on earlier rounds of testing, and so on. At key intervals, your strategy-making team should reflect on what it's learning and brainstorm changes to improve chances of success.

The PBS KIDS 24/7 strategy mostly involved packaging and distributing content already known to member stations, so the team did only minimal and informal testing of that, mostly by discussing sample programming schedules with other leaders. But the incorporation of gaming and digital streaming products was much more experimental, and the team created some simple prototypes to help network executives understand and critique the concept and to test it with target audiences. The team also leveraged existing research funded by the US Department of Education's Ready to Learn grant, which validated the educational benefits of combining broadcast programs with game play linked to the same learning goals.

Avoid indecision

Testing, learning, and evolving a strategy must not, however, become an excuse for extended indecision. As a leader you must be both open to new ideas but also committed to action. You can't develop strategic options forever. At some point, you have to freeze the code and commit to a strategy, or risk losing valuable momentum. Thus, at PBS, after a year of development and testing, Kerger and the team officially launched PBS KIDS 24/7 in partnership with member stations.

That's not to say you shouldn't still seek learning and improvement even after a strategy has been rolled out; it's always right to correct missteps and refine improvements over time. But after the initial process of development and testing, teams need a clear signal to move ahead and commit to coordinated action. Finding the right time to do that—knowing when you've not only analyzed enough but also done enough real-world testing to shake out remaining practical problems and adapt accordingly—and then having the courage to move forward is the critical purview of the leader. As you develop strategy, watch for the right window to make that decision.

Step 6. Allocate resources and manage implementation

The clearest signal that you are truly launching a strategy is when you begin to allocate resources and build implementation into your operational processes. This, too, requires some advance thinking and preparation. Toward the end of any strategy-making process, you will have to do more detailed financial and organizational modeling—analyzing the investment and people needed, additions or modifications of infrastructure, changes in organizational structure and responsibilities, and so on.

Once you've agreed on a final strategy, you and your team must build the choices and decisions into existing systems for your company: you must integrate funding, cost allocations, and expected revenue (as appropriate) into your budgeting process. You must accommodate any new recruiting and training within your company's HR systems. You must introduce any new operational, technology, and infrastructure requirements of the strategy into other functions as appropriate (for more details, see chapters 3 and 4).

But throwing the implementation switch is not purely mechanical. You as the leader must also ensure that your organization embraces and pursues the new strategy in a way that generates the results you hope for. To do that, you'll want to pay special attention that the strategy is managed for the highest possible performance—focused clearly on appropriately aggressive goals, well integrated into performance reviews, freed from what may be constraining barriers in the structure and culture of your organization, and similar (more on this in chapter 4).

In addition to providing for the operational integration of implementation, there are a few additional steps you should consider to get your strategy off on the right foot and build critical early momentum.

Focus investment

Planning and testing is always easier than finally committing to the public launch of something new. Once you give the green light, you might be on the way to becoming a hero, but even a promising strategy might fall flat and open you up to criticism or worse. But when you're ready, have the courage to move forward and accept the consequences, because unless you enter the game, you will certainly be seen as a failure. Too many leaders undermine their chances of success by flinching at the moment of execution.

Anne Mulcahy, again reflecting on her Xerox turnaround, emphasized the importance of considering resource allocation as a leader: "Much of the leadership I had to exercise was fighting to secure the right funding and people needed for the new initiatives. Leaders often don't want to expose themselves to failure by making the hard decisions, so they suboptimize and put a little money here, a little money there, and nothing has enough oomph to break through. Those decisions are really difficult, because inevitably you're taking money away from one group to support another."

As implementation starts to move ahead, you'll also have to keep enforcing discipline on what the unit has to stop doing to maintain the focus of your strategy. Just because everyone seemed to agree in this or that workshop about making a major shift, or shutting down this or that older initiative, doesn't mean they will follow through on their promises. Institutions are hard to change, and the anchor of tradition and what's familiar can be very heavy. PBS, in order to pay for the new dedicated children's channel, had to postpone the launch of new individual shows and undertake some organizational restructuring. Kerger had to make and enforce what were ultimately some difficult decisions.

Communicate clearly

Any strategy-development process will have its share of complexity. Your job as a leader is also to simplify and communicate your choices about where and how the team will now play—and why. Everyone in the unit and other stakeholders (colleagues in the organization, board members, customers, investors, partners, etc.) must understand what the strategy intends, why specific goals are targets, and how the team will achieve them. Keep your key messages short, powerful, and easy to understand; they should clearly connect strategy to the vision and mission. Repeat them constantly, in every interaction you have with your stakeholders, and make clear what the strategy will mean for each of them. (The discussion and experimentation you've had along the way will mean that the key tenets will not be surprising, but they will still need to be constantly reinforced.)

Mulcahy engaged the people at Xerox constantly during the company's strategic transformation. As she met with stakeholders worldwide, she always explained how their particular work could help the company's strategic efforts. By staying away from conceptual executive speak and addressing the implications for change in a targeted, practical way, she was able to make the strategic transformation personally meaningful.

At PBS, Kerger continues to allocate significant time to promoting PBS KIDS to the system and a wide range of stakeholders—speaking candidly and personally about the importance of the strategy and its fit with her vision and the broader educational mission of PBS. She is methodical in reaching out to different leaders across the organization, her board, station managers, and other community leaders in the PBS network. She also now regularly references PBS KIDS 24/7 in her outreach to current and future donors across the system.

Keep learning, keep adapting

The notion that strategies must be continuously renewed is not new, but the pressure on organizations to do that is harsher than ever before. The rise of lean and learn-by-doing approaches to strategy reflect a new generation of organizations finding ways to adapt to a more volatile and competitive climate. To help with the shift, they are using new technologies to collect and analyze large amounts of customer and market data, including, in real time, enabling faster tailoring of product or service offerings as change unfolds.

Similarly, at PBS, the national office monitors viewership progress of the new children's channel and continues to collect feedback through audience data analysis and ongoing discussions with local station leaders. It has integrated PBS KIDS 24/7 into regular planning and operations for all PBS national units, and managers continue to work with content producers and curriculum advisers to refine the various offerings.

As a leader, you should embrace such tools, but don't confuse technology with human judgment or assume that more data analytics is all you need: if you're going to keep your strategy fresh and relevant, you must keep challenging the organization with these questions: Why is a particular strategy working or not? Why are changes in markets opening up new problems or opportunities? What, in fact, does that mean for our strategy now—and tomorrow? Leaders lead strategy making by leading the learning that must continuously shape it, while also looking to reinvent it periodically through more dramatic innovation over time. (For more on this, see chapter 5.)

Are you ready to lead a strategy-making process?

Kerger brought good judgment and a willingness to help a passionate, bottom-up, cross-functional team succeed in its development of a successful new kids' channel strategy. The team members' willingness to collaborate and learn from each other, plus some fortuitous timing and even a little luck, all contributed to that success. In the end, however, the most critical factor was the disciplined problem-solving and iterative learning approach Kerger encouraged the team to follow. Its analysis of markets and opportunities, engagement with other leaders and experts across the system, and then the continual refinement and improvement of the concept that it developed over the course of a year allowed PBS to navigate key strategic choices about where and how to create new and distinctive value within its educational mission.

If you are an emerging leader in a larger organization, be alert to strategy-making opportunities to build your knowledge and skills. You might be invited—or raise your hand—to develop strategy for a new product or create a localized strategy to start a process of innovation or some broader transformation for your firm. Or you may have a chance to develop a strategy outside the boundaries of a traditional corporate structure, for example, with a consortium of partners working on a collaborative venture, or to help launch a new experimental initiative or social advocacy program your company is sponsoring. Every opportunity to develop new forms of value, requiring informed choices about where and how to compete within a particular domain, and then turning those choices into well-aligned action, can provide you with valuable experience—teaching you how to work toward your vision and achieve impact through the focused power of people working together.

Questions to Consider

- **Starting point.** Do you have a strategy for your unit or team that supports the company's current vision and overall strategy? Is it clear what your team needs to do—or not do—in order to really make a difference? Is there good reason to rethink your strategy now? If so, can you articulate success and then set goals for a new strategy?

- **Audience.** Who is the audience for your team's strategy—your boss, the senior executive team, your customers, other parts of your organization, your employees, or all of the above? How can you align these stakeholders, particularly if they have different expectations?

- **Key issues and challenges.** What current challenges are facing your team? Are external threats or changes in markets, technology, or competition pressuring your business? What internal challenges are you also facing? Are you competing with others for talent or budget? How will you sharpen your understanding of these issues? Are you doing things that don't add value and you should stop?

- **Opportunities.** What opportunities does your team or unit have for adding significant new value to your organization and your customers? Are there services or products that you can provide better, faster, or cheaper than anyone else? What's the distinct value that you can bring that will differentiate your team from others? Is there data that can help you confirm these opportunities?

- **New thinking.** What new, creative approaches can you take to improve your team's work and increase the impact of your team's contributions? Are there new products or services to offer? How can you tap into your team's wisdom and experience to identify new opportunities?

- **Options and choices.** What choices about what to do and what not to do should be the basis of your team's strategy? How might these play out and what would it take to move in each direction? Are certain options more distinctive and harder for competitors to follow? Do certain options fit better with your company and skills, and lay a foundation for more future growth? How can you quickly test your preferred options with customers, executives, and other stakeholders and then use the data to iterate and improve your strategy?

- **Allocate resources.** What are the resource implications of your team's strategy? Do you need more budget or different capabilities? Are you giving your team members the resources they need to be successful?

- **Implementation.** How will you assign accountability and track progress of your team's strategy? How can you do this in a way that allows for continual learning, midcourse corrections, and the development of sustaining capability?

3.

Getting Great People on Board

I believe the real difference between success and failure in a corporation can be very often traced to the question of how well the organization brings out the great energies and talents of its people.

—Thomas J. Watson Jr.

In chapter 2, we talked about how to translate your team's vision into a tangible and measurable strategy to address an environment with changing technology, market opportunities, and customer needs. To execute the strategy, however, you need to get the right people on board. After all, a key part of our definition of leadership is that much of your impact is through others. That means building a leadership team and an organization with the best talent and the right skills for executing your strategy, and motivating them to do so to the best of their abilities.

To do this, you need to achieve a fine balance between putting the organization's needs first while also respecting the needs and desires of your staff as they pursue their professional and personal aspirations. People join organizations voluntarily, with the assumption that their participation is a two-way street. If they give their best efforts to achieve the collective goals that you lay out, they expect to be rewarded, in terms of compensation, growth, job satisfaction, relationships, and more. This is the basic social contract of organizational life, and when it works, your team is more likely to perform at a high level with committed, loyal, and motivated people.

As a leader, you are the creator and steward of this social contract, whether for the whole organization or your part of it; thus you need to honor both sides as you make decisions about staffing, organizational structure, development, and compensation. Good leaders don't obsessively drive for performance goals in ruthless ways that leave a trail of bodies (or unhappy people) in their wake. But they also aren't so concerned about making everybody happy that they avoid conflicts and hard decisions and end up not achieving the needed results. Good leaders thread the needle between these extremes so that the organization has the right people on board to execute strategy and get results—*and* they feel good about being part of the collective endeavor.

But threading this needle can be challenging. Frequently, the individual's and the organization's interests can seem misaligned. What happens if, in order to achieve your strategic goals, you need to lay someone off or fire them? What if they want to be paid more than you can give? And developing people by giving them tough feedback can be in the best interest of both the individual and the overall company, but it still isn't pleasant or easy. Engagement is hard to pin down; not everyone is motivated by the same things. Convincing people to change or grow can be difficult; culture is deeply rooted in organizations. And managing the social contract for your whole department or unit is challenging when most of your interactions are primarily with your direct reports, and it just seems that so many of these things might be easier to hand off to human resources.

To confront these challenges, your particular focus as a leader needs to be on building your direct reports into a strong team of results-producing leaders and managers who also understand and honor the social contract, and can multiply your commitment to it through the rest of your organization. Doing this includes five elements:

- Finding the right mix of leaders and managers to work directly with you to execute the strategy and helping those people work together effectively, across functions and silos

- Ensuring that your direct reports get the feedback they need to either get better at their jobs or make the decision to go elsewhere, and that they do the same with their people

- Creating opportunities for great people to learn, grow, and develop

- Articulating an explicit incentives philosophy that motivates your direct reports and all of your people to do the right things, for both the organization and themselves

- Combining these steps into an organizational or team culture that can enable strategic change

To start, let's look at a case that illustrates the tension between achieving organizational objectives and honoring individual aspirations.

Managing the social contract through strategic change at the Ford Foundation

When Darren Walker became president of the Ford Foundation in 2013, he identified a new strategy for achieving the organization's vision of reducing inequality and injustice, strengthening democratic values, promoting international cooperation, and advancing human achievement: the foundation would have to take a more digitally focused approach to its work. Walker explained: "The rise of the digitally connected world presents a threat to social justice that we hadn't been aware of, such as internet freedom and net neutrality, the creation of open and free access platforms, and the challenge of a single lane internet vs. fast lanes given to the wealthy. In addition, all of the things in an analog world that are discriminatory and unjust, like bullying, wage inequality, and predatory lending, are replicated in the digital world."

As Walker dug deeper into this issue, he realized that many of the people reporting to him, and others below them, were not well prepared to tackle these issues. It wasn't a matter of motivation or commitment, but rather one of understanding and skill. There were few digital natives on the foundation's staff, much less the executive team. Walker thus faced a challenge: despite good will on both sides, there was a gap between the strategic needs of the organization and the capability of its people to carry it out. Walker's job as leader was to close the gap as quickly as possible.

Walker considered his options. Should he ratchet down his strategic expectations to match what his people could do? He didn't see this as a viable option, since that would weaken the effectiveness and competitive position of the foundation. Another equally unappealing option was to replace many long-standing, highly committed, and loyal staff with new digitally savvy people who could quickly grasp the new strategic agenda. But that would compromise current programs, create negative publicity, and destroy remaining and future employees' faith in the social contract that they had signed up for, destroying morale and productivity in the process. Walker was also aware that firing people for no fault of their own would breach the very principles of social justice that the foundation stood for. Walker was firm on this point: "How do you stand before the staff and say to many of them who came to the foundation because they had the skill to work in social justice, that they are missing a critical skill needed to work on social justice in the twenty-first century?"

Walker found a third option, however, that allowed him to meet *both* the organizational and the people sides of the equation as much as possible. The solution involved a careful combination of the options: some new hires, some staff reductions, and retention of a significant number of current staff, but with changing expectations supported by development and retraining, extensive performance feedback, and new goals and incentives. "Technology fellows" were new hires introduced into each program area. These digital technologists had the task of rapidly familiarizing existing program staff with the digital world. Walker and his team also changed the job descriptions for new program officers to require some experience with coding and a basic knowledge of the digital landscape in addition to their own field. Finally, they changed the actual programs to focus on creating a new field of internet rights, marrying human rights to understanding technology and media, and lots more.

Though this solution proved to be a good one, it was still a wrenching and difficult change for the organization and for Walker, particularly since he knew that not everyone could make the shift successfully. But he was clear and candid in his communications: "I had to deliver a tough-love message, saying to people that while we had a lot to be proud of, if we continued on that path, a lot of them would be irrelevant. I also had to be frank about the fact that some of them wouldn't make it. It wasn't easy."

Assembling your leadership team

Walker's story demonstrates how difficult it is to get the right skills and capabilities to pursue your strategic goals, while also respecting everyone's security and well-being. But the reality is that just as strategy development is a continuous process, you will need to be continually making related staffing decisions. That's true at the scale of the whole organization, and particularly within your own department or team.

Every leader, at every level, needs to have a top-notch team to help develop and then execute strategy, and drive the organization forward. But the direct report team is especially important because its work cascades down to everything else the department or organization does. Sometimes you'll need to recruit the team or part of it, but most of the time, you'll inherit a team already in place. As Walker did with his leaders, you'll need to make sure that all members of the team have the capability to fulfill their particular roles and collaborate with others as needed in order to achieve the organization's goals.

So what are the most important things to consider when looking for the right people for your leadership team? And how do you assess whether those you already have can make the cut?

Recruit the right leaders

As you consider your team of direct reports, you'll need to create a list of critical attributes that reflect what you think will be most important for executing your strategy and getting things done. For example, ConAgra's former CEO Gary Rodkin made a list that included technical excellence, vulnerability, the ability to communicate and develop people, time management, and basic people skills. You also should look for skills that allow your team members themselves to be great leaders of their own teams (see more on this in the section "Build Your Team and Coordinate an Organization of Teams" later in this chapter). We believe that two such skills are particularly important across sectors and industries at all levels: adaptability and emotional intelligence.

Claudio Fernández-Aráoz, a senior fellow at the Harvard Business School and an experienced recruiting professional, provides useful guidance on recruiting adaptable leaders in his HBR article "21st-Century Talent Spotting." Fernández-Aráoz argues that rather than technical skill or specific knowledge, the most critical characteristic that leaders should look for in selecting people is *potential*, "the ability to adapt to and grow into increasingly complex roles and environments." This approach recognizes the pace of change in a global, digital world in which the skills and competencies important in the past might not be relevant for future challenges.

Emotional intelligence is also increasingly seen as critical for leaders across functions, especially as organizations become flatter and managing in a collaborative way becomes more crucial. Daniel Goleman and his colleagues' pioneering research has shown that leaders who are aware of their and others' emotions and who are able to moderate their own emotional responses also have more ability to create great organizations and teams. (Goleman and his coauthors describe the hallmarks of emotional leadership in their classic HBR articles "What Makes a Leader?" and "Primal Leadership: The Hidden Driver of Great Performance.")

Finding people who meet your criteria doesn't mean that all your direct reports need to look alike, act alike, or think alike. Recruiting people with complementary and diverse skills is equally important. As a leader, you must mix and match talents, backgrounds, and tendencies (including your own) in a way that will allow your team to succeed collectively. So as you build your team, assess current strengths and backgrounds. Are there any that are missing? Who in your organization might have those qualities? Also look at personality types to make sure you have a mix of people who are different enough to spark creative thought, but still able to collaborate.

Venture investor Bob Proctor compares this process to constructing a dynamic jigsaw puzzle. He spends much of his time making sure that the startup companies in his portfolio have leadership teams with the right mix of skills and thought processes, and that the companies' leadership recognizes who's good at what and builds roles around them and what they excel in. You can do this formally as you build or develop your team by using one of the personality-style assessment tools available in the market. Although none of them is perfect, they provide interesting insights into different ways that people approach problems, communicate, and think. You also can get the measure of current and potential team members by giving them problems to solve, asking them to make a presentation, conducting role-plays, or finding ways to have them interact with other members of your team. All these methods will give you more insight than just checking résumés and conducting one-on-one interviews.

As you focus on other members of your team, also pay particular attention to your own gaps. Anne Mulcahy, the former turnaround CEO of Xerox whom we met in chapters 1 and 2, for example, did not consider herself to be a very strong strategist. Most of her career had been in sales and operations, so her strengths were in people and communications. When she became CEO, she realized that strategic capability would be critical, so she made sure that at least two other senior executives had those skills when putting together her leadership team.

Make the tough decisions

Identifying the right people for your leadership team also goes hand in hand with identifying those team members who should no longer remain. Jack Welch, the legendary former CEO of GE, used to say that leaders need to be "hard-headed and soft-hearted." As a leader, you need to be totally

How solid is the social contract on your team?

The tension between achieving strategic goals and honoring the social contract exists at every level of the organization and isn't just an issue for CEOs and senior leaders. Team members expect that in return for their best efforts, they will receive compensation; have opportunities to grow, learn, advance, and build relationships; and have a safe, stimulating work environment. At the same time, as their leader, you expect them to put their heart and soul into the work and produce great results.

In many instances, however, the pressures and demands of getting work done and the expectations and performance of team members don't fully match, and the fabric of the social contract begins to fray. As a leader, you need to look out for the warning signs of that happening so that you can take action as early as possible. These warning signs might include:

- People on your team worrying about getting credit or recognition for their contributions, which can signal that people don't feel adequately rewarded

dispassionate about getting the right people in place in order to implement your strategy and get results, but still be personally compassionate about how those choices affect the individuals involved.

This means that if one of your direct reports isn't working out—they're not the right fit, or they're not performing despite whatever guidance and support you've given them—you need to take them off the team. That may not necessarily mean letting them go; you may be able to find a role that is a better fit for their skills elsewhere in the organization. Finding the right place for them is a compassionate way of removing them from the team, but so is being candid about exactly where they didn't perform so that they can improve, either at another position in your firm or elsewhere. Letting them stay and continue to fail or feel uncomfortable, however, is *not* com-

- Team members competing for plum assignments, complaining that they are not getting sufficient opportunities, or actively looking for other jobs, which may suggest a lack of development options

- Increasing backlogs of work without a clear sense of how to get it all done or problems with quality or ability to meet commitments, which may mean that some of your people are not up to the task or you don't have sufficient resources

- Conflicts between team members, either openly or in passive-aggressive ways, which may indicate that the social and working environment is not healthy

- Withholding information others need to succeed or setting others up for failure, which can be signs of a toxic workplace

As a leader, you can't always make everyone happy while achieving your goals, but you can watch for indicators that the social contract isn't working. So take a look at your team and ask yourself whether the social contract is being met or is showing signs of wear and tear.

passionate, is not upholding your end of the social contract, and is actually doing a disservice to that person and to the rest of your team. (For more on how the social contract can play out on a team level, see the box "How solid is the social contract on your team?")

What does the combination of dispassion and compassion look like? Years ago, Welch asked one of his top leaders to come to his office during the week between Christmas and New Year's Day. The leader, who ran a multibillion-dollar business and had met his revenue and profitability targets for the year, thought that the meeting was going to be about his bonus or possibly even a promotion to run one of GE's larger units. Instead, Welch told him that he was being let go because his leadership style was autocratic and based on fear, completely contrary to GE's values. Welch had told him this numerous times in the past year, but he hadn't taken it seriously. After some tough discussion, the business leader accepted the rationale for his departure and saw it as a wake-up call. He went on to become the CEO of another company where he paid a great deal of attention to more effectively balancing his top-down, results-producing style with the growth and well-being of his team. In retrospect, he later said that this experience, despite the pain, was one of the best learning moments of his career.

Building, fine-tuning, and maintaining your leadership team is a continuous challenge. Strategies change. Customer needs evolve. Markets shift and new technologies emerge. And often people—at all levels of the organization—cannot adapt to the changes in their environment. Adjusting for this starts with the people who report to you.

Build your team and coordinate an organization of teams

Once you have the right people on your staff, you still have to put them together to form a team. Building a high-performing leadership team doesn't usually happen by itself, however. You can't just put a collection of talented people in a room, lock the door, and wait for a cohesive group to emerge. As a leader, you have to actively help your direct reports come together.

This is vital because your people are likely to have greater impact by working together and because teamwork is a critical part of the social contract. Most research shows that people's satisfaction at work is determined not only by what they do, but also by whom they do it with—both their immediate supervisor and their coworkers, whether they belong to lower-level teams or more senior leadership teams. So having productive, supportive, and collaborative relationships between your direct reports is a key factor in ensuring that your people are motivated, engaged, and committed to your vision and strategy. Building this kind of teamwork also multiplies your impact. For example, the shift to a digital mindset at the Ford Foundation ultimately was not driven by Walker alone, but by his senior leaders as well.

Coalescing strong and capable individuals into a high-performance team takes work. As a leader, you must do so deliberately. Based on years of research into team performance, Martine Haas and Mark Mortensen suggest four key steps in their HBR article "The Secrets of Great Teamwork":

1. Ensure that your team has one or more *common and compelling goals* that require everyone to contribute in some way. At the Ford Foundation, the senior team was collectively responsible for driving a digital mindset into every program and aspect of the foundation's work. To make that happen, all of the senior leaders had to not only take action within their own areas, but also look at the implications across programs and functions, and act as an overall steering group for the transition to digital.

2. Create an *agreed-on structure* for how the team will work together, including norms of behavior, sharing information, when and how to hold meetings, communication patterns, and clarity of assignments. This doesn't mean that you dictate to everyone how the team will work, but rather that you discuss these issues with your team explicitly so that the structure becomes solidified.

3. Provide the *support* needed for the team to succeed, such as education, access to resources, budgets, coaching, and the like. At the Ford Foundation, the provision of digital fellows to senior team members is a good example. Support, however, also means psychological support so that your team members feel that they can get help and constructive feedback from each other rather than attacks and put-downs.

4. Foster a *shared mindset and sense of identity* with the team. Particularly in organizations where team members may be dispersed, traveling frequently, and connecting virtually, you need to encourage people to develop personal relationships and get to know each other beyond just the immediate tasks and roles. Find time for off-site sessions, unstructured discussions, dinners, and occasional fun activities, sometimes including spouses and significant others—all of which can help bring your team together.

Your team of direct reports, however, is not likely to constitute the only team in your scope of responsibility. Your direct reports may also have teams reporting to them and so forth down the line. So the way your direct team operates can create a model for the others.

Furthermore, your organization probably also has many cross-functional teams for product development, customer service, systems introductions, and the like. In addition, your firm might have occasional or standing teams that include people from outside organizations, such as open innovation forums or corporate social responsibility initiatives, and you may run or participate in some of these. As a leader, you need to ensure that the multiple teams that constitute your organizational ecosystem are functioning together as well as possible. (See the box "The importance of thinking horizontally.")

New patterns of flexible and agile interactions between these kinds of networks of teams have recently been reinforced by General Stanley Mc-Chrystal, former commander of US Special Forces in Afghanistan (see his book, *Team of Teams*). McChrystal emphasizes that traditional top-down leadership is no longer effective in warfare when the enemy is a decentralized network that changes strategies and tactics almost instantaneously. Instead, troops on the ground have to understand the overriding mission that they are to accomplish, have all the information and training possible, and then have the freedom to make their own decisions in the context of the mission. Moreover, these troops have to operate not only as effective teams on their own, but also as teams of teams that can coordinate their efforts with other units rapidly and flexibly.

These lessons apply to all types of organizations that operate in fast-changing, unpredictable environments, which is almost every organization. As a team or department leader, you should:

- Encourage your team of direct reports to interact, share information, collaborate, and support other teams beyond those that report to them directly. Don't assume that teams in different silos will naturally collaborate with each other, no matter

The importance of thinking horizontally

Your team is probably situated within an organization that includes many other teams from business units, technical groups, and support functions. The other teams can be in different locations or could belong to outsourced partners, and they all might have their own identities, goals, priorities, and work patterns. Part of your job as a leader is to help your team members work horizontally with these other teams, even if they don't report to you. To do that, you need to periodically ask yourself the following questions:

- What other teams do we need to work with in order to have an impact and get things done? (To answer this, you might draw a map of your organization's ecosystem and where your team fits in it and discuss this with your team.)

- What do we need from these other teams and how does that fit into their priorities? Conversely, what do they need from us? How aligned are we in how to go about this work together?

- What's the best way to make sure we all get on the same page? Should I meet regularly with the leaders of the other teams? Should we bring the teams together in some sort of working session or Work-Out?

how much they are committed to the goals and have the right information.

- Reinforce to your team members, and have them reinforce to *their* teams, that all their individual decisions need to actively and directly help move the organization toward the strategic goals you have identified. Your vision and strategy practices come into play here as well, especially the efforts you make through those practices to ensure that everyone understands your unifying direction and strategic objectives.

- In addition to communicating your vision and strategy, push as much information as possible down to all your teams in order for them to make the best possible decisions. The more they know, the better they will be able to find the right ways to collaborate with other teams in the service of achieving the strategic goals.

For example, to help his teams communicate with each other, Welch challenged GE to become a "boundaryless organization" in which information and resources could move quickly up and down the hierarchy, across functions and business units, and between the company and its customers and suppliers. To make this happen, Welch required all his senior leaders to sponsor and participate in two-day "Work-Out" sessions where people from different parts of the organization, regardless of title or pay grade, came together to quickly solve business problems. Sessions also were held between GE and its customers and suppliers. The Work-Outs—which GE and many other companies still hold—not only produced untold millions of dollars in business benefits, but also taught previously siloed teams how to work together without waiting for the boss to bring them together.

Creating your team and coordinating a network of teams are key steps for navigating the balancing act between organizational success and individual satisfaction. Talented people thrive in an environment where they can effectively and easily work with others either day to day or as needed and feel that they are making a difference. And the more these people thrive and leverage their skills, the more successful your organization will be.

Harnessing performance feedback

Another key element in bringing people on board to execute your strategy is making sure that everyone knows how they are doing, so that they can continually improve and grow. We saw this at the Ford Foundation: Walker used performance feedback to help develop the digital capabilities of existing staff as the organization's strategy evolved. Without feedback, individuals and teams won't get signals that tell them whether their day-to-day efforts are working or not, or how to change. This is a key way of fulfilling the social contract by ensuring that people understand what it takes to succeed or whether another organization might be a better fit.

Giving constructive, candid, and timely feedback to subordinates is taught in just about every management curriculum. But even experienced leaders struggle with it, particularly because of the anxiety that it triggers. Looking another person in the eye and telling them how they are doing (whether good or bad) is difficult, and even more so when it might affect the person's livelihood or career. So we tend to avoid doing it, do it awkwardly, or slough it off to human resources. However, giving feedback is an even more critical skill for leaders than managers, because leaders are not only responsible for providing feedback to their own direct reports, but also for setting the tone for feedback and learning for the organization. It's a key part of having broader impact; as Mark Benjamin, when he was president of NCR Corporation, told us: "If I don't set the tone properly about giving candid feedback, the problem multiplies itself exponentially. There are 33,000 people at seven levels below me, and if I don't do it well, it could mean that there is someone on my team, who might have 4,000 people reporting to him, that doesn't do it well. So then the bar is lowered for all of those people."

Of course, you might not have thousands of people in your organization. But even if you and your direct reports are responsible for only a few dozen, each one needs to knows how they are doing. Just as the vision and strategy you set cascade down through your direct reports to others in your area, the way you give performance feedback also creates patterns beyond your immediate team. So not only must you give feedback to your direct reports effectively, but they must also do the same with their people.

Get through with tough feedback

For feedback to be effective, you need to think through the process and message beforehand and prepare yourself psychologically. Feedback can't be done well on the fly or in a hurried and frenzied conversation, no matter how busy you are. Sure, there will be times when it's appropriate to give feedback in the moment in response to a particular incident, but even then you should take a deep breath to think before you speak. As a leader, your words carry extra weight, and if you are overly negative, you can crush a person's spirit and self-confidence. So keep in mind a few principles:

- The act of giving feedback is first and foremost a business activity that's important for the health of the organization—to make sure people are doing the right things in the right ways. As Vito Corleone said in *The Godfather*, "It's not personal, it's business." The goal is not to make the other person feel bad, or to put them down, or to make yourself feel powerful. Rather, it's about making the other person successful so that you can achieve your organizational goals. And if someone can't be successful in their current role, then it's in both of your best interests to help the person find another role where they can succeed, either in your organization or elsewhere.

- Because feedback has a business purpose, frame the discussion as a problem-solving exercise rather than just telling someone what to do differently. Given current performance or personal behaviors, how can the person do better? What can they do? What can you do to help? What other resources could you make available? And what are the specific steps for moving forward, and over what period of time? Structure the dialogue so that it's a two-way street where you define the problem and invite both parties to suggest solutions.

- Base the feedback discussion on data and not just subjective impressions. Look at the results the person has achieved versus their goals, get views from other people who the person works with, and refer to critical incidents or specific examples to back up your message. Feedback should not be just your opinion.

Just as with any other skill, you need to practice, practice, practice. Giving tough and constructive feedback doesn't come easily for most leaders, so you have to find your own voice. Try writing out what you want to say or at least how you want to start. Role-play the dialogue with a trusted colleague or human resource person. Be clear about what you want the discussion to accomplish (an improvement plan, a better understanding of what's expected, a decision to change roles, etc.). Then assess afterward how well you did and what you could have done better.

In addition to individual discussions, one of the most powerful ways to deliver tough feedback so that an individual can hear it is with 360-degree feedback, which provides comments from multiple sources—boss, peers, subordinates, customers, and others. This assessment is particularly powerful because if common themes from a number of others don't align with a person's own view, those themes become more difficult to dismiss or ignore. Richard Ober, CEO of the New Hampshire Charitable Foundation, described the effect: "One of our key people was a brilliant problem solver and project manager, but did not have much experience leading people, and the culture in her group was strained. We did a 360 assessment to identify her core capabilities and weaknesses. She was stunned to hear reactions of people about working with her. I took advantage of her openness to listen to start intensively coaching her to evolve from being great at doing to being great at empowering. Now she's one of the best performers on our senior team and consistently gets very high rankings on annual employee surveys."

There will be times when people don't respond to individual feedback, however, and don't develop the way you need them to. When you've exhausted ways of discussing with them what needs to change, you may have to take action, letting them go from your team, as we described earlier in this chapter.

Team feedback

Feedback is not just a tool for improving the performance of an individual; you also should give feedback to your team about how they are performing together, and you should encourage the team members to give feedback to each other. For example, Jim Ziolkowski, the head of a nonprofit called buildOn, brings his leadership team together at the end of every year for a four-day session where they talk about how well each person and department achieved their key performance indicators for the year. Each leader prepares a brief summary of what they did well, where they fell short, and what they need to do differently in the next year, after which all the other team members give their comments and suggestions. They also talk about how their performances affect each other and how they can support each other going forward.

Leaders should give performance feedback to entire organizations at times, particularly about key performance themes or issues. Walker's challenge to the Ford Foundation about becoming more digitally savvy is a great example of this. Often this is the beginning of significant transformation and improvement for your organization, which we'll talk about in chapter 5. The point, however, is that feedback is essential not only for individual change, but for collective change as well.

Feedback throughout the organization

Giving feedback effectively to your own people models the behavior for others in your division or unit. But you also must build regular processes into the rhythm of the organization to make sure it happens regularly. Most large organizations already have a performance management system setting defined times throughout the year for employee assessment. These conversations often culminate in decisions about promotions, compensation, and development needs.

As a leader within that system, you need to meet the requirements of this enterprise cadence and also put your own stamp on it. That's the difference between your team seeing performance management as an onerous corporate process and seeing it as one that drives real business value. For example, the leader of a sales team within a large technology firm set up monthly talent talks with each of her direct reports and a quarterly talent talk with the group as a way of reinforcing the importance of keeping a focus on performance issues, both good and bad, and doing something about them. Then, when it was time to fill out the yearly corporate performance management forms and participate in the associated meetings, she and her team were already well prepared.

Of course, if you are leading a startup or a nonprofit, or taking over an organization, you may need to construct a broader cadence yourself. Just make sure that it fits your needs and encourages constructive feedback, and don't just delegate the creation of this system to human resources. For example, Dan Springer, CEO of DocuSign, insists that each manager have a performance discussion with their people twice each year, talking about what they are trying to achieve and what they are doing for the customer, the company, and the team. To compel his managers to actually do these well, he asks them to create a brief, one-page summary of the discussion and send it directly to him. He then reads all of them and randomly sends notes back to managers with comments about the reviews, sometimes asking them to do the review again if it didn't seem to have been truly productive.

Strategy consulting firm Boston Consulting Group (BCG) has another approach. In addition to immediate feedback on projects, BCG has a formal yearly process of written reviews for each of the 1,000-plus partners in the firm. These reviews are discussed in face-to-face meetings of the top twenty-seven senior leaders during partner performance week and are used to make decisions about bonuses, promotions, future assignments, and key development goals, which are then discussed with partners one on one. According to BCG's president and CEO Richard Lesser, this process gives the top leaders an understanding of talent across the organization and reinforces a "one firm" culture with consistent messaging. It also helps those leaders calibrate their own contributions with the many impressive performances outside their own areas, keeping them grounded and focused on supporting the next generation.

As your department or unit gets larger or you get more responsibility and the pace of work increases, you also should make sure that your performance management system doesn't become overly bureaucratic and begin to lose its value of driving systematic feedback and improvement. For example, Raghu Krishnamoorthy, senior vice president and chief human resource officer at GE, notes in HBR's "The Secret Ingredient in GE's Talent-Review System" that GE's leaders (up to and including the CEO) routinely spend 30 percent of their time on people issues, including having intensive debates on individual performance evaluations. To get better re-turn from that time, GE is working toward creating digital tools to make this process more streamlined and flexible so that these discussions can happen when they are needed, not just at certain times of the year. Profes-sional services firm Deloitte also is reinventing its performance manage-ment process and reducing the time involved by focusing more on quarterly performance snapshots than on yearly evaluations. Marcus Buckingham and Ashley Goodall describe this transformation in more detail in their HBR article "Reinventing Performance Management."

The result of an intense, candid, and transparent feedback process during the course of the year is that staff throughout the organization, and your team specifically, know where they stand and how they have to im-prove. It also weeds out weak performers or those that no longer fit with your team, department, or the organization. Equally important, it gives you a solid basis for assigning people to new opportunities or roles.

Fostering learning and development

Giving your direct reports feedback and creating a system for feedback throughout the organization is one way to foster the employee growth you need to meet your strategic goals. More formal learning and development is another way. By giving your direct reports and aspiring leaders resources for personal and career improvement so that they can better meet the orga-nization's needs, you are also giving your people the ability to adjust, grow, and thrive to meet their own goals—an important part of fulfilling the so-cial contract. For example, look again at the Ford Foundation: Walker was able to help his program managers learn to understand the digital world by hiring technology fellows. Thus, he was able to keep many of these em-ployees on board, while they equipped themselves to perform well in other future roles.

Your human resource function likely focuses on this kind of develop-ment specifically, but you have a role as a leader as well. By putting some of your own time into the talent development of your team and creating stretch opportunities for your best performers, you can drive your vision and strategy and give everyone the sense that you take your employees' career growth seriously, which can be a major selling point in attracting even more good talent.

Put your time into top talent

Jack Welch used to say that he only had two ways of making an impact on GE: one was to allocate financial resources differentially, and the other was to ensure that his various business units had the best possible leaders to take advantage of that financial capital. To make that happen, Welch spent a huge amount of personal time reviewing and sharpening leadership succession plans and decisions, interacting with promising leaders, and conveying messages about leadership themes to various groups inside and outside the company.

How involved you should be in talent development depends on your personality as well as the size, scope, nature, and maturity of your organization or unit. But you do need to be personally involved to some degree; this can't just be delegated to human resources or consultants. After all, you are in the best position to connect the vision and strategy with the talent development plan. And when you're directly involved, you send a message to all other managers and employees that development is a serious business endeavor and not just a nice perk to make people happy.

One way to structure your involvement is by participating in the talent and leadership planning review process like Welch. Another way is by personally participating in special events, programs, and training sessions with your team members. Often senior people feel that development sessions are just for lower-level people, and if they participate at all, it's just a ritual appearance or speech. Joining in more intensively, however, can be a powerful opportunity to get to know your team members and future leaders, share your views about what's important, and send a signal that learning and development is for everyone.

For example, shortly after Kenneth Frazier became the CEO of biopharmaceutical company Merck, his human resource team organized a series of development sessions for high-potential leaders (fifty at a time) in conjunction with a prominent business school. Frazier met with the designers of the program to ensure that his views about what leaders needed to do to make Merck successful were incorporated. But Frazier didn't stop there. In addition, he personally attended the two-day programs from beginning to end as a full participant, engaging in small-group and plenary discussions throughout. This gave him direct exposure to dozens of potential leaders whom he hadn't known before and gave him a platform to share his vision for the company and what it needed to do strategically. His participation also sent a strong signal to the participants, and the thousands of people who reported to them, that Frazier was committed not only to Merck's long-term success, but to theirs as well, which is the essence of the social contract.

Leaders don't need to spend all their time sitting through leadership development programs. But you should take a hard look at your calendar and at how much time you are devoting to the review and development of your department's or team's talent. For many leaders, business, customer, and competitive pressures often squeeze out the time for direct involvement in the development of their people. If you let this happen, however, you may end up with people who won't be able to help you reach your goals.

Stretch your high potentials

Another way that you can personally give your team members opportunities to grow is to force people into assignments and projects that will stretch their abilities beyond what they think might be possible.

Most research on talent development shows that leaders learn much more from real situations in which they are forced to get things done than they do from case studies, simulations, and training sessions. Harvard Business School professor Michael Beer and his colleagues have pointed out for years that leadership training on its own—roughly a $350 billion business (as of 2015)—has little impact on real leadership performance (for more, see their HBR article "Why Leadership Training Fails, and What to Do About It"). As a leader, you can create challenges for your direct reports, and if you are a senior leader, you can make sure that these kinds of opportunities are available to high-potential people throughout the organization.

You can create these kinds of experiences for your team members by:

- **Giving your direct reports tougher and broader goals.** For example, McKinsey Global managing partner Dominic Barton describes what happened when he was tossed into the deep water early in his professional life:

  > The key to my career was when I was asked to head up the McKinsey office in Korea. We had eighty people but weren't considered to be a prominent firm in Korea and didn't really have a way to grow. The orthodox wisdom, I was told by my predecessor, was to keep a low profile, not be in the media, and not talk to newspapers. But if we were so quiet, how would any Korean companies know about us? So I took a risk and started to write a short newspaper column every week about business and management issues. It was published in Korean, so I knew that nobody at McKinsey outside of Korea would read it and I couldn't get caught. Eventually, these columns helped me get to know the fifty people who really matter in Korea, build relationships with them, and grow our practice. In essence, I had a small playground to work in and try new stuff.

- **Asking your people to work together to achieve something.** For example, the president of a large academic medical center asked his top twenty leaders to jointly address the changing health-care landscape and find ways to put the institution on more solid financial footing. These leaders, who ran various clinical departments, research areas, and operational functions, were all experts in their fields, but had little experience leading strategic change, nor had they developed their skills at working across disciplines. They tended to be protective of their own areas and budgets. By taking on this joint assignment, however, the leaders were forced to take an institutional perspective and think about trade-offs between areas. They brought in experts on health-care trends to educate them on the external environment and learned how to do a SWOT-style analysis on their own organization. Over the course of several months, they identified a number of strategic initiatives and financial shifts and took responsibility for getting them organized and carried out. In addition to the institutional results, the effort helped the leaders develop new skills and perspectives. One eventually became the interim president, and another became the chief operating officer—roles that they would never have been able to handle without this experience.

- **Moving people into stretch assignments.** You and your HR partner can set this up in a number of ways, such as through project-based training or special projects. In project-based training, high-potential leaders from different areas are given a specific project to achieve over a two- to three-month period (while continuing their regular jobs) and learn skills needed to accomplish the project through focused workshops, webinars, or work with a leadership coach. Siemens, for example, used this approach for many years to not only accomplish substantial results (such as introducing products into new countries), but also to develop hundreds of next-generation leaders. And if your organization doesn't offer training like this, you can take the initiative by giving your people special projects on your own and support their learning with online, university-based, or consulting inputs. For example, the head of a marketing team challenged one of her high potentials to organize a new recruiting process for the team and sent him to a university program on human capital to get some fresh perspectives.

- **Creating job rotations.** Another approach is to rotate your people through different parts of the company so that they have hands-on experience with a variety of business challenges, cultures, and geographies. International Paper, for example, moves its high-potential leaders across units and geographies to give them a broader perspective on the company and to see how they perform under different conditions. If your company doesn't do this routinely, you can work with colleagues to trade good people or just champion some of your people for open positions. Some leaders hesitate to do this because they fear losing good people from their team, but if you don't actively help them find new opportunities, the best people will do it on their own, and you might lose them from the organization completely. The other advantage of actively helping your people move is that you will then have a network of former team members throughout the organization who can collaborate with you and support you in the future.

While all these approaches to development sound straightforward and sensible, many leaders still hesitate to act on them. After all, it takes work, time, and money to develop people, and if you do a really good job, the person might still go to another team or another company anyway where they can get more money or responsibility. Great people will always have other opportunities. So why should we make the investment and watch someone else reap the returns?

Unfortunately, there is no easy answer to this question. Great leaders, however, understand that it is ultimately less expensive and far more effective to develop their own talent than to constantly bring in outsiders who will need to go through a learning curve and who might not work out in the end. Internal people usually have a far greater chance of success and become productive much more quickly. So in the long run, developing talent will pay off many times over, both in productivity and in reinforcing the social contract of your organization.

Sharing your incentives philosophy

Not all people are alike. They have different motivations for coming to work and different long-term career aspirations. At the same time, the actual work that they do is not always comparable. So how do you reward everyone for their performance in a way that they feel is fair and equitable, *and* that attracts, retains, and develops the kind of talent you need—*and* doesn't break the bank? Questions of incentives always get to the heart of the social contract: your compensation framework must address all these competing concerns.

Many leaders simply try to avoid these questions by creating or perpetuating undifferentiated compensation systems ("just give everyone a 5 percent raise"), by staying away from career discussions with their people, or by just turning compensation over to human resources. And while that may ease their discomfort, it rarely creates high-performing organizations, because it means that good people often end up going elsewhere.

Instead, your role as a leader is to articulate a philosophy of incentives clearly so that people know what it takes to be successful—whoever they are and whatever their goals.

Make your incentive philosophy explicit

Your job as a leader is not to get into the business of designing compensation and benefits plans. There are hundreds of expert consultants and firms that can do this work for you, along with your own human resource team, whether you're a startup or a multibillion-dollar organization. But in order for these experts to put together a plan that will help you achieve business results *and* make people feel good about being part of your team, you do need to provide some clear direction for how to decide on salaries and bonuses, award promotions, and confer other benefits. That is what we call a "philosophy of incentives."

Even if you are not in a position to drive an incentives approach for the whole organization, by sketching out a philosophy of incentives for your department or unit (based on the organizational rewards system), you'll make your people aware of what behaviors and outcomes will be rewarded and recognized, and what it will take to advance in their careers, and, conversely, what behaviors or results will have adverse implications for their careers. Without that clarity, employees and managers will make their own decisions about what's best to do, and it might not actually be what you want or intend.

Steve Kerr, an expert on reward systems and the first chief learning officer for GE and then Goldman Sachs, in the HBR article "The Best-Laid Incentive Plans," describes "the folly of rewarding A while hoping for B."

The classic case of this is when a leader rewards and promotes people based on achieving individual goals, while assuming (or hoping) that these people will work together for the greater good of the team. But if their individual goals conflict with each other in some way, it's likely that they will compete with each other rather than collaborate, not because they are ornery, but because most people will rationally do what's in their own best interest first.

By making your incentives philosophy explicit, you send a clear message to your people about what you expect of them. For example, Andrew Géczy, the CEO of Terra Firma, a private equity firm in Europe, and a former executive at Lloyds and ANZ banks, explained to us that part of his incentives philosophy is that people's behaviors (and not just their performance results) are a key factor for compensation and promotion. He uses a two-dimensional grid for performance assessment with behaviors on one axis and results on the other. By making this clear to his organization, he prevents his managers from using tactics to get results in the short term that could harm the organization in the longer run.

Questions to ask

As you articulate your incentives philosophy, here are a few questions that you should address:

- To what extent are you committed to making sure that your team truly functions as a meritocracy, where individual achievement is rewarded versus just tenure, loyalty, or personal relationships? (Some leaders talk about results being paramount, but then reward people differently.)

- Is tenure rewarded at all (and if so, how)?

- What's the balance between individual achievement and collective achievement? In other words, should your team members be rewarded if they hit their individual goals, but the team misses its targets? Or should there be a portion of individual rewards that is based on the collective results—and that perhaps will differ for senior versus junior people? What about vice versa—what happens if the team or organization does well but individuals miss? Should they share in the rewards anyway? What is the weight on the individual versus organizational success?

- What behaviors are critical for success on your team? How seriously will you assess and compare these with the achievement of goals? What happens if someone does a fantastic job of reaching their business targets, but falls short in the behavioral sphere? Will you follow Jack Welch's lead and ask that person to leave despite the good results? Will you give them a second chance?

- What kinds of nonmonetary rewards can you provide as recognition for work well done? In addition to personal praise, to what extent can you use your communications channels to recognize people and make them heroes? Are there opportunities for managers and teams to present their achievements to others? Should you reward exceptional contributors through dinners, trips, or outings? What other ways can you make your team and top performers feel truly appreciated?

Obviously, every leader will answer these questions differently, and some will be applicable for the entire organization while others will apply at certain levels. Senior leaders, of course, have more influence over the entire incentives approach. But even if you are a team leader, you need to know how your organization thinks about these questions so that you can communicate them to your people. You also need to think about whether you can have some local control over some of the incentives. For example, there might be some companywide behaviors that are encouraged and rewarded, but you may have some additional behaviors that you want your team to follow. Similarly, there might be nonfinancial incentives that all leaders in the organization use, but there may be others that you develop yourself for your team (e.g., dinners with people who make special contributions).

Once you are clear about the answers to these questions (whether you are making the decisions yourself or more senior leaders are giving them to you), you need to communicate them to your team. Sometimes these are well understood or may be part of an employee handbook and on-boarding orientation. Usually, however, the incentives philosophy is somewhat opaque, with people making assumptions about what it takes to be rewarded or to get ahead. And in the absence of common understanding, people will be surprised, disappointed, or hurt when they receive their compensation decisions or talk with you about their career prospects. On the other hand, if you do make the basis for incentives as clear as possible, your people will have a pretty good idea ahead of time what to expect and will know what they need to do in order to do better.

In short, your job as a leader is to make the principles of rewards and incentives as clear as possible. Talk to your team as a group about the philosophy and what it means. Then talk to each person individually, long before compensation or reward decisions are made or announced, about how the philosophy applies to them. Is there a behavior that they need to work on? Do they need to temper their expectations for a raise because the overall company is not doing so well? Do they need to gain some other kind of experience in order to advance to a higher level?

The key point is that everyone in the organization needs to know the principles and how they apply to them. Even more importantly, once these principles are articulated, they need to be followed. If you and other leaders are seen as talking a good game, but not following through, it will damage your credibility and diminish people's commitment to your organization.

Shaping a culture for executing your strategy

Culture is one of those words that is used all of the time, but its meaning is not always clear. The dictionary definition is that an organization's culture is the sum of attitudes, beliefs, customs, and behaviors that distinguish one group from another. That culture develops over time as groups of people work together and create repeated patterns and habits. Eventually these patterns become informal rules or norms that most people in the group adhere to, and to which new members have to adapt. In this way, organizational culture has intense power to promote certain behaviors and actions.

Culture also is a key factor in people's decisions about whether to be a party to the social contract of your team—that is, whether your unit will be a place where they can meet their personal needs. And if the culture turns out not to be a good fit with their expectations or abilities, people might opt out.

Managing your team's culture is thus a powerful way to determine how effectively your people execute on your vision and translate your strategy into action. If your new vision or strategy is generally in accord with the culture, then change can happen quickly. But if the current culture is at odds with the kind of strategic change you are proposing, it can be a true roadblock. That's why many CEOs are fond of saying that "culture trumps strategy," a truism that Jon Katzenbach and his coauthors explain in their HBR article "Cultural Change That Sticks."

The main problem with managing culture, however, is that it's invisible, implicit, and hard to describe. If you ask ten people in your company or team to portray your culture, you'll probably get ten different answers because everyone sees it from their own perspective. In addition, every organization has subcultures, perhaps in geographies (how things are done in a particular office) or functions (R&D works differently than finance), or in units that were bolted on through acquisitions (but retained their old cultures).

Perhaps you can't change your team's or organization's culture completely or quickly, but you can try to get some key aspects of culture to work for you instead of against you. To do so:

- First, make your cultural goals explicit to your direct reports and their people.

- Then, use the elements already described in this chapter to move people toward those goals.

Define your cultural goals

It's not up to us to say what your team's culture should be or how you should try to shape it. That's a decision that you and your team should make, based on your vision and the strategy that you are trying to execute. Given the increasing pace of competitive and technological innovation, however, many organizations are trying to create cultures that are specifically more agile, open to change, and quick to align themselves with new ideas. If that's the case for you, then your cultural goals should reflect these shifts and/or others that are important.

To make your cultural goals explicit, work with your direct reports. First, discuss the key cultural characteristics that currently exist in your organization or group. You can use an assessment like the one in figure 3-1, which defines some basic areas of organizational culture, to prompt your discussion. You may want to add some other areas that pertain specifically to the strategy you are pursuing, such as digital savvy (as in the Ford Foundation example) or openness to partnerships.

Next, consider how you might need your team's culture to be different in order to support and drive your particular strategic goals. Where are the biggest score gaps? As you work, continue to iterate this dialogue with other groups and ask your direct reports to hold similar sessions with their teams. Since culture is the accumulation of behaviors across an organization, you can't just dictate it from the top down. You also have to engage people at other levels so that they buy into and help shape the cultural shifts and make them come alive.

For example, the head of a small factory within a large corporation became frustrated when he learned that most of the plant's productivity-improvement projects, all of which his team had ratified, were delayed. As he dug into the situation, he realized that the problem was not lack of skills, know-how, or resources, but an inability of his direct reports to make decisions (at all stages of the projects) without him. Since he was too busy to attend every project meeting, many decisions were simply not made. In talking with his team about this pattern, he realized that this was a cultural issue: his team members were hesitant to take risks, and he had not truly empowered them to do so, which made him the decision-making bottleneck. As this pattern became clear, the plant manager began to pull himself out of each decision, and as issues came up, he repeatedly told his direct reports to use their best judgment and do what they thought best. At first, his people hesitated (or didn't believe him) and kept going back to

FIGURE 3-1

Assessing culture

*Instructions: Place an **X** where you are today and a **XX** where you need to be*

	1	2	3	4	5	Gap
1. Decision making		Authority to make decisions centralized at top		Authority to make decisions dispersed throughout the company		
2. Business information		Information about business and strategy reserved for senior management		Information about business and strategy available to everyone		
3. Communication style		Formally through written memos and official meetings		Informally through conversations and impromptu meetings		
4. Employee expertise		People encouraged to focus on functional expertise and a single job		People encouraged to develop many skills for a variety of jobs		
5. External relations		Company has traditional contractual relationships with customers and suppliers		Company develops formal and informal partnerships with customers and suppliers		
6. Solutions sharing		New ideas and solutions infrequently shared with other departments		New ideas and solutions regularly shared throughout entire organization		
7. Rewards		Rewards and responsibility based on title or tenure		Rewards and responsibility based on accomplishments		
8. Work behavior		Company encourages and recognizes individual performance		Company uses teams and recognizes teamwork		
9. Work orientation		Emphasis placed on defined work processes and roles		Emphasis placed on getting measurable, bottom-line results		
10. Innovation		Employees use traditional and tested approaches to getting the work done		Employees looking for and experimenting with innovative ways of getting work done		

Total gap _____

ask him what to do. But over the course of several months, as he repeatedly refused to make the decisions for them and kept pushing them to do
it themselves, the culture started to change. And as team members made
their own decisions and the culture began to shift, delivery times on the
projects dramatically improved.

Identifying cultural shifts or priorities is important at all levels of the
organization. At GE in the 1990s, Jack Welch saw that the company was
highly bureaucratic, slow moving, hierarchical, complex, and overly analytical. He and his leadership team emphasized "speed, simplicity, and self-
confidence" as three cultural characteristics that he wanted to encourage,
and that they saw as critical for GE's success in the twenty-first century.

When Ken Frazier became the CEO of Merck, he did something similar. At the time, Merck was in the final stages of integrating its purchase of
Schering-Plough Pharmaceuticals, and the combination of the two companies had created a very large but overly complex and slow-to-decide enterprise. To counter this, Frazier set cultural goals focused on the principles of
"prioritize" (focus on what's important), "align" (collaborate with others to
get these important things done), and "simplify" (find the most direct and
least complex ways of doing them).

Shift the culture

Naturally, it's not enough to just state some desired cultural shifts. You also
have to take action to move your organization toward them. While there
are powerful symbolic acts you can perform to model the culture (see the
box "Symbolic actions to model cultural behaviors"), the other elements of
managing people we describe in this chapter also constitute deeper ways
to set a culture shift in motion.

Build your leadership team

If you have some clear cultural shifts in mind, then you can look for people
who tend to work in those ways, just as Darren Walker actively recruited
new program managers with more digital savvy and who could work more
effectively in a digital world. If someone on your team does not exemplify
your cultural goals, you may need to let them go, as Welch did with the

Symbolic actions to model cultural behaviors

As a leader, you can have an outsized influence on your organization's culture by modeling the behaviors that you want to encourage. A study by Angelo Kinicki and Chad Hartnell (described in Alison Beard's article "CEOs Shouldn't Try to Embody Their Firms' Culture") found that CEOs in the best-performing organizations actually behave differently from the prevailing culture because their job is to bring new ways of working to the table. They note, "Leadership styles are contagious. So, if a CEO [who wants to drive more discipline around results] . . . does strategy and implementation reviews with his top team every other week for a year, it will have a trickle-down effect and eventually change the culture of the whole enterprise."

Leaders also can influence organizational culture through small, subtle, and even symbolic actions. Jack Welch used to send personal, handwritten notecards to employees as a way of reinforcing and recognizing particular behaviors that he wanted to encourage. Robert Galvin, former CEO of Motorola, often would have his lunch in the employee cafeteria to signal that executives were accessible and wanted to listen. The new president of a large financial firm that we worked with prominently displayed a "no whining" sign in her office to reinforce her emphasis on solving problems and not just complaining about them—a message that quickly circulated through the ranks. Other executives we've seen have used their personal involvement in nonprofit causes as a way of encouraging their people to give back.

One reality of being a leader is that people infer messages and signals from your behavior, whether you intend to convey these or not. Anne Mulcahy of Xerox told us that one of the toughest things about being a CEO is that she had to be "always on," and even things she said or ways she acted in unguarded moments could be interpreted as important. The downside is that the bad behavior of a leader (insensitivity, abuse, lack of accountability) can create a license for everyone else to act that way, which can lead to an extremely dysfunctional culture. The upside, however, is that the impact of your positive behaviors can multiply many times over.

high-performing business leader who was out of step with Welch's goals for the culture. This incident sent reverberations throughout GE that cultural behaviors mattered and would be factored into promotions, rewards, and advancement. Years later, many people still feel that that moment was the turning point for changing GE's culture.

As you manage how all your teams work together, ask them to think a few minutes about their own cultures and how they are working, and what they can do differently going forward to move toward the cultural goals you have set.

Harness performance feedback

Performance feedback is a more obvious way of shifting culture-related behavior. To use it this way, however, you need to be very clear in your feedback about the desired cultural behaviors and the gaps that might exist, and you need to do this without pulling punches. In most organizations that have shifted their cultures, this kind of brutal honesty is critical. You should also include questions about a person's cultural fit in their 360-degree evaluations.

Foster career development

While you create opportunities for people to grow and develop, and advance in their careers, you can simultaneously help them understand, internalize, and act on the cultural goals that will enable your strategy. For example, in the high-potential leadership development sessions at Merck, Ken Frazier not only talked about his vision and strategy for the company, but also about how having a culture of prioritize, align, and simplify would help make it happen. During the sessions, Frazier and the faculty (including other Merck executives) also facilitated specific discussions about how these leaders could apply the cultural principles to their day-to-day work, and each made specific commitments to do so. You can also make job rotations and stretch assignments with the explicit expectation that these will be opportunities for the leader to learn new behaviors, not just get exposed to a different business or geography.

Offer incentives

Positive reinforcement of cultural behaviors is powerful. When organizational members see that the people who are rewarded, promoted, and recognized are those who exhibit the desired cultural behaviors, it provides a strong incentive to also act in those ways. You also can reinforce the desired behaviors by selecting people for key assignments who already have those behaviors, or who have the potential to do so.

Putting this all together, of course, takes a lot of hard work and isn't accomplished overnight. Over the long term, however, building a culture that helps you advance your strategic goals, and that people feel good about, can have an enormous impact on your organization and can reinforce the social contract. It also can be incredibly rewarding for you as a leader. When reflecting on his tenure as dean of Haas Business School at the University of California, Berkeley, Richard Lyons told us that aligning the school with a concise set of cultural principles was perhaps the most significant thing he had achieved because it had become such a key factor in attracting students and faculty to the school. Shaping the culture also shaped his legacy: "It has put heart and soul into the institution that will outlive me."

The practices we've described throughout this chapter are not sequential steps, nor one-off activities. Instead, in order to create a high-achievement and high-morale organization, you need to continually practice these elements, determining the right way to approach them as your organization continues to change. Bringing people on board to support your vision and strategy requires constantly assessing and adjusting these different elements over time.

But done well, you can attract talent for years to come. Mastering the steps we've described and creating a culture that blends both organizational and personal success is hard work, and many of the associated skills for doing this may not come naturally. Taking some of these actions may also require uncomfortable discussions, such as when you need to be tough about performance feedback or promotions or rewards. Getting the right balance between organizational and personal success may not win you any popularity contests. But in the long run, it will be one of the keys to unlocking your own leadership potential and generating the significant impact that makes a difference for your organization.

But to achieve that impact, you need to enable this motivated team and staff to generate results. In chapter 4, we'll talk about how to make that happen.

Questions to Consider

- **Your team.** What skills and capabilities do you need within your team of direct reports? Does the team meet your expectations, or do you need to make some changes?

- **Fostering teamwork.** Are you satisfied with how well you and your direct reports function as a team? Do you have shared goals, agreed-on ways of working, and a common mindset? Do your team members help each other to be successful, and do they foster a "team of teams" approach that prevents silos from getting in the way of doing good work? Do they work to promote and extend the right kind of values and performance behaviors throughout the organization?

- **Performance feedback.** How faithfully do you give brutally honest but constructive feedback to your team members? How well do the members of your team give candid performance feedback to their direct reports?

- **Developing talent.** Are you spending enough time on developing the skills and capabilities of your team members? What do they aspire to achieve in their careers? How does each of them need to develop in order to be successful, and how you can stretch them to do that?

- **Incentives.** Have you made it clear to your team members what it takes to be rewarded and recognized, both individually and collectively?

- **Culture.** What cultural characteristics do you want your team to exhibit? How well are you modeling this culture with your own behavior?

4.

Focusing on Results

Effective leadership is not about making speeches or being liked; leadership is defined by results, not attributes.

—Peter Drucker

Organizations exist to produce collective results that individuals cannot achieve alone, whether revenues, profits, innovative products, or contributions to society. As a leader looking to make an impact, you need to take specific actions to ensure that those results follow from your team's ongoing efforts.

Unfortunately, many leaders make the mistake of thinking that getting results is simply the by-product of the other leadership practices that we've described. They focus on creating a vision, building a smart strategy, and getting the right people on board and spend much less time considering whether those activities are adding up to the highest level of performance possible for their organization or team. But to achieve that high performance, you need to focus on results specifically. When you absolutely have to achieve results, it forces you and your team to work differently and discover new opportunities that you never would have seen if you were not under the gun to deliver.

Focusing on results is not a sequential step that happens separately, after you have done the other practices. Rather, you can approach many aspects of your work—including the rest of these practices—with a results focus. For example, to get results, you have to make smart decisions about *how* to execute your strategy, and having a results focus can also inform the strategy itself, as we'll see in one leader's story. Focusing on results can also help you determine what people capabilities you need, while at the same time helping you develop those capabilities. And for a leader, your results should always be calibrated against the vision that you and your people are trying to bring to life.

In this chapter, we'll walk through the four elements that create a focus on results:

- Establishing high expectations for measurable business outcomes and holding people accountable for achieving them

- Reducing the organizational complexity that gets in the way of producing results

- Building your people's capabilities to get results, particularly when it requires new ways of working

- Maintaining execution discipline through regular metrics reporting and operational reviews

None of this is easy, of course. For many leaders, the skills necessary for the achievement of results don't come naturally, especially rigorously holding people accountable for their numbers and asking tough questions about operational performance. For anyone who is conflict averse, getting results involves mastering anxieties about confronting others and resolving differences. And to sell a set of high-performance goals, you need to be good at using a challenge to motivate people. Mastering this area, however, can be the difference between success and failure, not only for your organization or team, but also for your career—and theirs. The reality is that a track record of producing results will open up new opportunities for you more than anything else on your résumé.

To show you what it means to focus on results, we'll use the case of Seraina Macia, during an earlier phase of her career when she was CEO of XL Insurance's North American Property and Casualty Business. (She is now executive vice president at AIG.)

Focusing on results at XL Insurance

When Seraina Macia (then Seraina Maag) was recruited to become the CEO of the XL Insurance Group's North American property and casualty (P&C) business in 2010, it was, in her words, "an underperforming and shrinking business" with just under $800 million in premium revenues and a mediocre combined ratio (a measure of insurance company profitability). Macia's vision was not just to improve profitability but also to create a self-sustaining growth business that could win a significant share of the P&C market in North America, both of which would require an intense and unrelenting focus on achieving results.

Macia knew that she couldn't do this on her own; she needed to get her team focused on achieving better results as well. But many of them had been at XL for a long time, felt that they already were doing the best they could, and were skeptical that rapid growth was possible. Furthermore, the insurance experts worried that the unbridled pursuit of new premium revenue would require them to take on more risk, something that they felt strongly was the wrong thing to do. So her first challenge was to get her own team in sync with her expectations—and her results-driven way of thinking.

To get started, Macia brought her team together to analyze the data of the business. Its work revealed that the national market share of one of her units was higher than the others, which gave Macia hard evidence that significant improvement was possible. If one business could do it, then others could as well. Macia then established an aggressive, companywide, market share stretch goal based on this analysis.

She then required each member of her senior team to create specific, measurable, strategic growth plans showing how they would deliver their portion of the stretch goal. Some team members struggled with this; they were so focused on thinking about how the core business already worked that they simply weren't able to think creatively about how to redeploy XL's assets to meet a specific growth target. When they failed to deliver a workable plan, Macia held them accountable, and in a compassionate but tough way, she took some of the actions we described in the last chapter for replacing senior team members who weren't the right leaders for the organization.

Early in her tenure, Macia also recognized that there were some aspects of the organization's structure that made little sense for a group focused on improving business results: for example, the staff functions were more powerful than the business leaders whose units would do the work of reaching the stretch goal. She reorganized the structure of the business to have the business leaders report directly to her rather than through others, which allowed her to better focus on the growth plans that they were developing and would be held accountable for.

Macia also knew that the growth she was demanding would require many parts of the business to work in new ways. For example, one part of XL's growth plan indicated that new business would come in part from a change to a more proactive approach to finding new business rather than simply assessing proposals that brokers sent them. But that was a significant shift for underwriters and others. So to help them develop new patterns, she created five small teams (including underwriters) and charged them with winning new business in geographic markets that XL had not previously penetrated within 100 days, with thirty-day check-ins for all the teams. Through the process of trial and error, the teams learned about this new way of doing business and about the new geographical areas themselves. By the end of the 100 days, they had won their first new business and were well on their way to winning more.

Finally, Macia set up a disciplined system to monitor the ongoing operational performance of the organization. She identified the metrics to measure not only top-line results, but also aspects of the business that pointed to the health of her new initiatives and of the businesses' growth in particular. She set up employee progress updates, senior team meetings, and one-on-ones with her direct reports to hold candid discussions about these numbers on regular schedules.

Macia's focus on business results drove substantial growth. When she left XL after three years to take on a next challenge at AIG, the business already had climbed to around $1.8 billion in profitable revenue from premiums. Equally important, Macia had changed the culture of XL's business so that striving for the next level of performance was something that every manager was expected to do. A year after Macia had left, the leader who succeeded her (one of her previous direct reports) brought the business over the $3 billion threshold, an incredible achievement for a business that just a few years earlier had been underperforming and shrinking.

Setting high performance goals and holding people accountable

The first element of focusing on results is to set aggressive goals for your unit's performance, and to hold your team accountable for those goals. Whether you're setting a vision or a strategy, or executing on those initiatives, focusing your people on a specific, tangible goal creates a more immediate sense of urgency, especially if they know that failing to meet that goal has consequences. By focusing your team members on a stretch goal—rather than keeping their thinking embedded in how the business currently operates—you also free them up to think creatively about what to do differently to achieve it. And you'll learn quickly if they just don't have the ability to deliver.

Pushing those performance expectations ever higher meanwhile is one of the key ways that leaders can drive their teams toward more significant impact. As the late professor C. K. Prahalad once told us, the job of the leader is not to be a "caretaker" who maintains a steady level of performance, but rather a disruptor who pushes the organization to deliver more. If the leader doesn't play that role, according to Prahalad, they run the risk of becoming an "undertaker" for an organization that may not survive. Let's look more closely at how you can do this.

Ratchet up expectations

We've seen that setting high expectations is a critical leadership step for developing a vision (remember the BHAGs), creating a strategy (moving into new territory), and getting the best out of people (stretch assignments). It's also the essential starting point for improving results.

To set a challenging performance goal, start by identifying one or two key performance measures that can tell you whether your team or unit is moving toward your aspirational vision (or not). This could be a revenue or profitability number, or a measure of quality, cycle time, customer satisfaction, new product introduction, and so on. Then come up with a specific improvement target that will cause your people to gasp because it seems impossible. If you get that reaction, you're on the right track. You want people to realize that just doing more of what they are currently doing, or just working harder and longer, won't get them to the goal. Instead they'll need to work differently, smarter, and more creatively, and they'll have to figure that out along the way.

At the same time, of course, you shouldn't make the stretch goal so high or outlandish that your people will give up and not even try. So support your stretch goal with some evidence that success is possible—that others have achieved similar results, or that customers are in need of what you are offering. (For other ways to develop stretch goals, see the box "How do you develop a stretch goal for your team?")

For example, when Macia began at XL, she quickly brought her business and functional leaders together to look at the overall data about the business, which they had never done as a team. In that session, she pointed out that one of their eight P&C businesses had achieved a 3 percent share of the national market. Although modest, if all of the businesses could get to that level, their combined premium revenue would more than quadruple to over $3.2 billion. "Obviously," she told them, "we won't get to this number overnight. But significant growth is possible—we've proved it in one area—and we should aim for it over the next three years."

Macia acknowledged that the goal was going to be hard to reach. But she also expressed the strong belief that her people and the organization could pull it off. This combination of empathy ("We know it's a stretch") along with encouragement is important to get people charged up and motivated.

Along these lines, Macia also pointed out that XL had a lot going for it—a good reputation in the market, solid products, a large network of brokers, and strong technical expertise. So it had a lot of assets to work with; they just needed to figure out creative ways of using them in the service of growth. Macia emphasized, however, that she was not talking about just any growth, but rather targeted opportunities that would meet XL's underwriting and risk standards and would improve the all-important combined ratio.

On the surface, it sounds perfectly logical, even simplistic, that in order for people to achieve exceptional results, you have to ask for them explicitly. But as Robert Schaffer pointed out in a classic HBR article "Demand Better Results—and Get Them," the ability to establish high-performance expectations may be "the most universally underdeveloped" leadership skill in organizations. This is because human behavior often causes leaders unconsciously to shy away from making tough demands on their people for fear that they might be unable to succeed and you'll have to fire them, or that they might argue with you about the goals, or that they might want to trade off one goal for another. Indeed, as Macia told us of her initial conversation arguing for the performance goal she set, "My direct reports and my peers thought that I was entirely mad."

But making these tough demands can transform your organization or team. For Macia, the process of challenging her people to create a multibillion-dollar, profitable, and secure growth business was a seminal moment in the pursuit of results: if she had not pushed them to the next level with this seemingly crazy goal, the team would likely have continued doing what they had done before, with more or less the same results.

Making these types of results-focused demands also applies to leaders of functions or teams throughout the organization, not just to CEOs like Macia. Every group has the potential to be more productive and create greater value, but it won't happen unless they are challenged to step up their game by a demand-making leader.

How do you develop a stretch goal for your team?

If you want your team members to focus on a step-up result, you need to challenge them with a stretch goal. But how do you come up with the right one? Here are several approaches you can take:

- **Ask internal or external customers to identify something your team could do to help them be more successful.** For example, the head of an analytics team for a digital marketing company asked several sales managers whom she supported to consider this question. The most common answer was to identify which ad characteristics were most likely to be clicked through by different customer types—which would help them target sales more effectively. Based on these discussions, she then challenged her team to help the sales leaders increase click-through rates for four customer segments by 10 percent, using predictive models, over the next six months.

- **Ask your own people to identify their most intractable problems.** Using this approach, the head of a technical field services team learned that engineers were frustrated when they showed

Hold people accountable

Every leader talks about the importance of holding people accountable for meeting their measurable goals. Making it happen, however, is not so easy. Nobody wants to be viewed as (or feel) mean, unfair, unbending, or unreasonable, which is what often happens when you create meaningful consequences for not delivering, like withholding a bonus, slowing down promotions, moving a person to another role, or taking someone out of your organization altogether.

If you bend over backward to avoid these tough decisions, however, your people are less likely to deliver on the stretch goals. Human beings up at a job site that was not ready for them or didn't have the right equipment. Based on these inputs, the leader set a stretch goal for the year of having 95 percent of field sites ready to go when engineers arrived.

- **Predict a possible crisis.** At their core, crisis situations are stretch goals caused by external events such as natural disasters, competitive surprises, or strikes. Of course, you don't want this kind of emergency to actually happen, but you can think about the possibilities and use them as starting points for stretch goals. For example, what would you do if a storm knocked out one of your production lines? You would need a stretch goal of increasing production on your other factory lines to make up the difference. Or how would you cope if a major customer suddenly defected to a competitor? In that case, you might develop a stretch goal of accelerating your first-discussion-to-close rate by 30 percent to make up the difference.

Think about your team, department, or unit: what are some possible stretch goals that you could use to drive the focus on results?

have an almost infinite capacity to take credit for good results, but avoid responsibility for failure: they are able to give any number of excuses. As an IT project manager once told us, "We can use one bad weather day for many months as an excuse for being late with our deliverables." The trickiest thing about these rationalizations is that many are indeed true. Technology changes rapidly, and it's hard to realize the gains that were promised from it; competitors make unexpected moves that affect results; new regulations constrain your people's ability to take action; economic ups and downs make it impossible to plan; and the list goes on. The reality is that stuff happens. Holding your people accountable can feel like blaming them for things that are outside their control.

What makes it even harder is that most of the time your people truly are working diligently, putting in long hours and extra effort. Add in the fact that they probably are loyal and committed to you and the organization, may have been around a long time, and are critical contributors in lots of other ways. So, you rationalize to yourself, how can you take punitive action against such well-meaning subordinates? Instead, it makes more sense to give them another chance, empathize with all the difficulties, and reward them for effort rather than results.

As reasonable as this sounds, making this the standard way of dealing with your team will lead to a breakdown in accountability and likely failure in achieving your stretch goals. There may be some situations in which it might be the right thing to do, particularly with innovative, high-risk initiatives, new business startups, or truly unexpected situations. But on the whole, if some people are let off the hook, then everyone expects it. Eventually it becomes acceptable to try hard (or look like you're trying hard) but not deliver results, which means that mediocre performance becomes the norm. This isn't good for the organization and isn't healthy for your leadership. As Gary Rodkin, the former CEO of ConAgra, explained, "I can sleep at night only if I know that the commitments my people make are set in stone and that they will indeed deliver."

Instead, focusing on results means that you must evaluate your people on what they actually deliver. There is no A for effort. So you should be sympathetic to the challenges they are facing, the distractions they have to overcome, the organizational barriers, the bad weather, and everything else that makes it difficult to meet goals. And you should help them think through how to overcome these and what it will take to be successful. This is what Jack Welch called the "softhearted" part of making tough people decisions that we talked about in chapter 3. However, you can't wait too long to shift into the hardheaded part of this process. If they can't deliver, despite all the help, support, and encouragement, then you have to take action or they won't take the goals seriously. This is also part of the social contract that we discussed in chapter 3.

You don't have to don a Darth Vader costume and fire anyone on the spot if they don't meet their goals. You can give the person a specific milestone to hit in the next two weeks to help them get back on track or give them a short-term test to see if they can achieve a different goal. Another alternative is to pair the person up with a colleague or coach for a next assignment to see if they can learn how to produce more effectively. You also can move the person to another role in your organization where they might be more effective. Doing nothing, however, should not be one of your choices. Letting poor performance slide without consequences sends your whole team—and maybe your whole organization—the message that you are not serious about achieving results.

In the XL case, holding people accountable was indeed a critical issue for Macia, particularly since her predecessor had not enforced the delivery of results to a great extent. Even though their past numbers weren't great, she couldn't assume that the existing business leaders weren't capable of delivering, since nobody had ever held them to task. She had to give them a chance.

The first test that Macia laid out was for each of her senior business leaders to come up with a specific, measurable growth plan that would collectively move the business to her goal of $3 billion in high-quality premium revenue within three years. Asking them to work with their teams and figure out how to grow revenues profitably and without undue risk was a challenge in and of itself, something that the leaders had not done before. And as it turned out, a couple of the business leaders did not meet Macia's expectations. They did not think creatively enough, spur their teams to come up with new ideas, collaborate with functional support areas, or really contribute to Macia's overall team at the level she wanted. So instead of waiting, Macia quickly replaced them. As she said, "I saw what we needed and that some of the people weren't right for these jobs. I agonized about it but realized that I can only be as successful as the team around me."

Macia didn't just arbitrarily move people aside. While her business leaders were working on their plans, she held a series of candid discussions with each, talking about what she expected and what they were able to deliver. And when it became clear that a couple of them couldn't deliver, she took action. She then continued to do this as the direct reports executed their plans, very much like a short-term, turbocharged version of the performance feedback process that we discussed in the previous chapter. As she conducted these dialogues, during the next year, she ended up replacing a number of the business leaders because they couldn't achieve her ratcheted-up expectations for the organization. But that didn't mean she fired them; some she just moved to roles more suited to their skills. As Macia explained, "They weren't the right people for these jobs. But that doesn't mean that they weren't good people, or capable contributors, just that they didn't have the skills needed to deliver against the higher growth expectations."

Again, the process of holding people accountable for results is not just the purview of a CEO or senior executive. Leaders at all levels need to do this in order to create a culture of accountability and results delivery. If the people on your team don't achieve their goals, you won't succeed. And if you don't learn how to hold people accountable early in your career, you'll be less likely to advance. So while you might be unable to move team members elsewhere in the organization, you can conduct tough performance conversations, withhold bonus or promotion recommendations, shift people's roles and responsibilities within your team, and generally make it clear that delivering on results is nonnegotiable.

Reducing organizational complexity

As your people strive to meet the high goals you have set, they may uncover organizational barriers that get in their way—a reporting structure that means a team isn't incentivized to work with them or an outdated process that doesn't take into account new technologies, for example. Your team members will deal with some of these on their own; that's one way you'll find out how good they are and how much ability they have to be resilient and creative. But sometimes the barriers they uncover will require you, as their overall leader, to resolve or mitigate them because they cut across many groups and need someone with higher authority to resolve. Clearing away these barriers is the second element of focusing on results because it helps your people work together more simply and efficiently toward achieving those high-performance results and leading your organization to more significant impact.

In the HBR article "Simplicity-Minded Management," Ron describes four kinds of organizational complexity. It's up to you as a leader to simplify these types of complexity when they appear:

- **Structural mitosis:** changes in organizational design that get in the way of getting things done. You can address these by periodically examining your department's or unit's structure and adjusting it to make sure it serves the strategy you have set as simply as possible.

- **Product proliferation:** adding new products and services without taking any away or creating multiple variations of products or services. Run a portfolio review of your department's or team's offerings. Which are the most profitable or have the highest growth potential? Which best meet your customers' needs? Which yield diminishing returns? Which can be standardized? Eliminate or change those that no longer fit.

- **Process evolution:** ways of getting things done that are outmoded. To simplify overwrought processes, bring together many business stakeholders at different levels to redesign them from the ground up.

- **Managerial habits:** behaviors that get in the way of results. Invite your own team members to suggest how they could streamline their interactions with you. Perhaps you could delegate cross-functional issues more clearly, run meetings more effectively, or simplify your pattern of daily reporting.

All organizations suffer from different degrees of complexity in these areas. Your team may uncover some, but you should also do your own diagnosis of which need simplification, and in what order.

At XL, for example, Macia identified two key areas of complexity in her first months at the company, one having to do with the organizational structure and one with the evolution of the underwriting process. Because they both cut across the two divisions of the business that reported to her, property and casualty, Macia was the only person at XL who could do something about them. As a relative newcomer to the company, she was also uniquely able to identify them, since they had become part of the landscape over time and therefore were invisible to most of her team.

The structural issue emerged during Macia's very first meeting with her new direct reports. At the meeting, Macia realized that only two of the organization's eight business leaders (the heads of the property and casualty units) were represented at the table. Her other direct reports were all leading the company's support areas such as operations, finance, and human resources. "This is upside down," she recalls thinking. "While support functions are important, they aren't directly accountable for getting results." As she considered the issue further, she recognized that the organization's structure made the staff functions more powerful than the business leaders, so those support functions in effect were making decisions for the enterprise instead of enabling profitable growth. More concerning, the other business leaders, who oversaw auto, home, commercial, and other business units, reported to Macia only through the property and casualty heads. Based on this insight, Macia consolidated the support functions under a newly created chief operating officer position and elevated the other six business leaders to report directly to her along with the COO, the head of distribution, and the head of underwriting. This de-layering allowed her to focus more directly on the business leaders and the growth plans that they were developing and executing.

On the underwriting side, Macia also saw a major institutional barrier. The underwriting group had excellent technical skills in risk assessment and pricing. But Macia saw that the group's core process was focused inward: the underwriters waited for coverage proposals to come from brokers and then evaluated them using their strict technical criteria. Because of this process, XL ended up writing a very small percentage of the proposals that came to it and invested a lot of time assessing and rejecting the opportunities that weren't right for it.

Macia recognized that there were opportunities to improve this process. She organized a Work-Out session (like the one described in chapter 3) for underwriters and businesspeople to jointly figure out how to streamline the process so that they could instead spend their time moving into new territory to grow policy revenues, without creating undue risk for the company. The dialogue during the session revealed that the key was to get the underwriters away from their desks to actually work with brokers in the field. By doing this, they could jointly look for targeted new business that would meet underwriting standards in a more efficient way. So instead of underwriters waiting to see what the brokers would bring and then passing judgment, the underwriters could help develop standards about what brokers should look for regarding types of business, markets, geographies, and products.

For the underwriters at XL, this was a major cultural shift as well as a process change, but it was a critical factor in helping Macia achieve her aggressive revenue targets. Over time, as early results started to come in, underwriting became an enabler of growth instead of an anchor creating organizational drag.

Every organization, of course, has undue complexity that limits performance. Sometimes the complexity is baked into the culture and becomes invisible, as with the barriers that Macia dealt with at XL. At other times, the complexity is visible, but considered to be like a sacred cow that people can't do anything about. How well you eliminate or simplify it will dictate how quickly you can reach your business goals.

Building capabilities while growing results

High goals and organizational simplification won't help you improve your business results if your staff doesn't know how to do the work you need them to do. Increasing sales, for example, could be straightforward enough: make more sales calls, target different customers—these require the same skills. But more often, improving business results is not just a matter of working harder and doing more. Rather, it requires new approaches and smarter ways of working that may not be obvious. Increasing sales could also mean that your team should do more cross-selling, team selling, consultative selling, shifting to indirect sales, creating online or outbound sales, or some combination of them all. But what if the team has never done those things? It actually requires the sales teams to develop new capabilities.

The third element of leading with a results focus is to create opportunities for dozens, hundreds, or even thousands of people in the organization to learn how to work differently in order to get better results. Many leaders are tempted to dictate capability-related changes from the top down, which may sound like a logical approach. You can launch training programs to teach everyone new ways of working, and you can change compensation and promotion plans to provide the proper motivation, as you learned in the last chapter. Because you're the boss, you might assume that they will do what you say.

Unfortunately, it doesn't work that way, even in top-down organizations like the army. For example, General Stanley McCrystal, former head of Special Operations, emphasized, in the HBR interview "What Companies Can Learn from Military Teams," that effective operations in the army require clarity of mission, trust, and the continual development of team capabilities. It's not just about top-down direction. That doesn't mean that leaders can't provide resources and tools for learning. As we saw in the last chapter, Darren Walker gave his Ford Foundation program managers access to technology fellows to help them learn about the digital world. But the program managers themselves had to figure out how to take what they were learning from the fellows and apply it, in their own unique ways, to the social justice challenges in their programs. Building capabilities is not a paint-by-numbers exercise.

This is all the more true in nonmilitary settings. After years of research, Russell Eisenstat and colleagues concluded, in the HBR article "Why Change Programs Don't Produce Change," that the most effective change in organizations comes from bottom-up experiments in which managers and their people learn new capabilities and experience success, and then spread the new approaches to others. The leader, however, can stimulate the bottom-up experiments by demanding the achievement of stretch goals. When teams realize that they can't reach those goals by continuing to do what they did in the past, it forces them to search for new approaches.

To trigger these experiments intentionally, you can use an approach like one we've used called "rapid results initiatives," or RRIs, pioneered by Ron's former firm, Schaffer Consulting. In this approach, a leader sets up a structured process for empowering small teams of managers and employees to take an element of the company's growth strategy and generate real results in 100 days. As they do this, the teams figure out on their own what it takes to execute the strategy and achieve results. They experiment, try things, fail fast, and iterate toward what works. In the course of doing that, they build their own capability and the company's to make it happen.

As an example, at XL, one of the key elements in Macia's growth strategy was to target specific geographic markets that would be fertile ground for its P&C products. To carry out this strategy of proactively finding new business rather than letting business come to it, the organization had to develop new capabilities: how to identify key market opportunities; how to educate brokers about XL's products and partner with them in finding new business; how to collaborate across business lines; how to better leverage underwriting time and cost on the best opportunities instead of assessing everything; and more.

To develop these capabilities at scale and deliver results at the same time, Macia commissioned five RRI teams. She gave each team the challenge of winning new business in a geographic market that XL had not previously penetrated, such as Kansas City or St. Louis, and to get first results (measurable premium dollars) in 100 days. The team members included underwriters, representatives from the eight business lines, distribution people (who oversaw the broker network), and others.

During the 100-day period, the teams experimented with different approaches to achieving their goals and quickly began to learn what worked and what did not. To capture and disseminate these learnings, Macia brought the teams together at thirty-day intervals to check in on progress and share insights. These sessions also helped inject urgency and competition into the process as the more successful teams shared their early results with pride (for more on the power of these early victories, see the box "The power of small wins"). As Macia described, "We had the check-in conference call at thirty days, and one team was way behind. You don't want to be

The power of small wins

A critical aspect highlighted in Macia's work with RRIs is creating opportunities for staff to achieve small wins. Beyond giving your team low-risk ways of discovering and testing new approaches in real time, small wins give your team the confidence to try new things and break out of the old patterns of behavior (and levels of performance).

Harvard Business School professor Theresa Amabile and coauthor Steven Kramer describe these psychological benefits in the HBR article "The Power of Small Wins." Their research shows that making progress in meaningful work is the most important booster of emotions, motivations, and perceptions during a workday. The positive reinforcement of seeing progress gives us a sense that all our effort is worthwhile for more than just a paycheck. To counter that sense of malaise, many leaders feel that their job is to pat people on the back and encourage them to keep going. Unfortunately, without the visible evidence of real results, these well-meaning gestures often come across as veiled attempts to keep up the pressure. Instead, part of your job as a leader is to help your team achieve those real results, even in small doses, just as Macia's rapid-results teams gave people at XL a way of experiencing real success, quickly.

behind if you see everybody else succeeding. So there's a bit of competition going on, and at the next checkpoint the lagging team moved out in front."

At the same time, of course, the teams were learning what it took to drive growth proactively: how to identify the right brokers to work with, how to triage quotes that they had little chance of winning so that they had more time available for the business that they could win, how and when to bring underwriters and distribution people to the field, which materials would be most helpful for brokers, how to help brokers sell different lines of insurance to the same customers, how to work with brokers remotely when they didn't have a physical presence in the market, and more.

In addition to their newfound knowledge and skills, the teams achieved significant early results in the first 100 days, bringing in millions of dollars in new premium revenue. The teams then built on these initial successes and expanded them in the target cities, while Macia commissioned new RRI teams for other markets. As the process evolved, she asked one of her business leaders, Gary Kaplan, to oversee this effort and apply the RRI approach to other aspects of the growth strategy such as creating a new business to insure construction projects. In a two-year period, Macia launched over thirty RRI teams, engaging hundreds of XL people and generating hundreds of millions of dollars in new revenue while building new capabilities across the company.

Creating this kind of iterative learning cycle—with rapid tests of what works and how to fit pieces together—is a low-risk way of ensuring that your people really do deliver results. As Macia noted to us in our discussion about the RRI process at XL, "It won't fail. It's just not an option. We would take corrective action at the check-ins. We've had situations where teams have struggled in thirty days, but then you catch up with them so you can correct it."

Still, the iterative process can yield some challenging leadership dynamics: you can't completely control the outcomes because the teams will learn as they go along and most likely will come up with solutions and approaches that may be somewhat different from the original strategic plans. Fight your instincts and let this happen—in fact, encourage it. If you and your direct reports merely give teams rote instructions about how to proceed, they won't use their brains or reflect on their experience along the way. By empowering them to experiment as they learn, and learn from both failure and success, you'll allow them the flexibility to actually improve and enhance what was called for in the strategy.

Maintaining organizational discipline

The fourth element of focusing on results is to create and maintain a disciplined approach to monitoring the ongoing business performance of your unit. This involves choosing the right kind of metrics, establishing an effective operational cadence, and holding candid discussions about the results.

These activities may seem like standard managerial fare, but in a results-driven environment, they are particularly critical for leaders to attend to. Demanding adherence to high goals, removing complexity, and giving staff freedom to experiment and build their own capabilities can create a lot of energy and initiative. But without regular, disciplined attention to operational performance, you may find that individuals are reaching for their high goals in destructive ways, or that simplified processes aren't actually working as expected, or that changes to the strategy from the results of early experiments are getting out of control. A regular and rigorous system of diagnostic activities will help you monitor and maintain the health of your unit and make course corrections along the way.

Get the right metrics

At XL, as we saw, Macia and her team developed growth strategies for the eight P&C businesses. Metrics, however, made those strategies operational. As Macia described to us, "Behind the strategies we put specific plans in place and then we measured everything—old business, new business, cross-sell, and much more. What gets measured gets done."

Macia's comment about measuring everything is a bit of an exaggeration. Your real challenge as a leader is to make sure that the *right* things get measured, not everything. Organizations create lots of data: numbers, reports, trend lines, heat maps, graphs, spreadsheets—and these are complemented by external resources on call to produce onetime studies and answer specific questions. Most of the time, however, it's not clear that all this data is worth the cost and indeed leads to better business decisions and better tracking of performance progress. An important part of your job as a leader is to provide guidance about which measures and which data will make it possible for you and your team to know what's happening in your part of the business at any given time, while also acknowledging that there are times when you just won't have all the data and will still need to act anyway (see the box "Making decisions when you don't have all the data").

Making decisions when you don't have all the data

While it's critically important to have as much of the right data as possible to support your decision making, information will be lacking at times or you won't be able to get it on time, and you'll have to make a decision anyway. According to Ram Charan, a longtime adviser to senior executives and boards, more and more decisions will be made this way in the future. As the pace of change continues to increase, qualitative factors take greater precedence, and more and more variables come into play. In the face of this ambiguity, leaders can't always rely on analytics alone for key decisions, whether it's to enter a new market, acquire a company, try a new marketing approach, offer a new service to internal clients, or quickly respond to a customer problem.

When these situations arise, as they inevitably will, Charan suggests a number of ways that you can forge ahead in his HBR article "You Can't Be a Wimp—Make the Tough Calls." First, you need to sift through the information that you do have and select the few most critical factors that will truly matter in making the decision. Second, use your imagination to shape a few options—that we could do A, B, or C—and play out their implications. For example, if you tell customers that you will do A for them, what would be the impact on your bottom line or on the use of other resources? To what extent would it set a precedent? Would you have the capacity to honor this promise? How might competitors respond? What other second- or third-order effects might there be? Then, with these options in mind, toss them around with your team or some trusted colleagues, or even with an objective outsider. Encourage a spirited discussion of the risks and benefits. Make sure that you also look at the different scenarios from a customer or stakeholder perspective. And use whatever data you do have to help you clarify any of the choices.

(continued)

> Ultimately, you'll have to make a decision and trust your now well-informed intuition that it's the right one, or at least mostly right. You'll also have to back it up and be courageous in defending it, whether to more-senior leaders, customers, partners, or the board. As you do this, remember that making this kind of decision is probably better than trying to do more analysis and more data collection, which only kicks the can further down the road and delays getting anything done. And also remember that the more you learn how to make decisions without all the data, the better you'll become at doing it.

Part of this decision depends on your own inclinations. Some leaders want to base their decisions on as much hard data as possible. Others want just enough data to either reinforce or challenge their intuition. Still others may prefer a combination of hard, analytical data with anecdotal and qualitative input. But you'll also want to ask yourself and your team the following:

- **Are we focusing on the right questions?** Many companies collect the data that is available rather than the data needed to help make decisions and run the business. So you need to be clear about what questions you want your data to help you answer and then focus the data collection around that rather than everything else that is possible. Consider the key leverage points in the business or in your unit—the ones that will make the most difference between success and failure—and what data you need to track progress on these. Also think about changes that you are trying to foster and what data will tell you whether you're on track or not.

- **Does our data tell a story?** Most data comes in fragments. To be useful, these individual bits of information need to be put together into a coherent explanation of the business situation, which means integrating data into a "story." While enterprise data systems have been useful in driving consistent data definitions so that things can be added and compared, they don't automatically create the story. Instead, you should consider in advance what data you need to convey the story you need to tell—whether to your team, executives, shareholders, or customers—and give your team some direction about how to pull it together. Make sure, however, that you don't start with a preconceived story (or conclusion) and then look for data to support it, but rather let the data paint the picture.

- **Does our data help us look ahead rather than behind?** Most of the metrics that leaders review are retrospective. They tell you about performance in the past, but are less effective in predicting future performance. Therefore, it is important to ask what data, at what time frames, will help you and your people get ahead of the curve instead of just reacting.

- **Do we have a good mix of quantitative and qualitative data?** Neither quantitative nor qualitative data tells the whole story. For example, to make good product and pricing decisions, you need to know not only what is being sold to whom, but also why some products are selling more than others.

Clearly, business data and its analysis are critical for your department or organization to succeed, which is underscored by the fact that the business intelligence and analytics space is becoming a billion-dollar industry. But even the best-automated tools won't be effective unless you are clear about these four questions.

The challenge of establishing the right metrics applies not only to C-suite leaders, of course, but also to leaders of divisions, units, and teams, because without the right measures, it's like trying to fly a plane in the dark without an instrument panel. For example, the leader of ad sales for a digital marketing company was concerned that sales numbers had plateaued, despite the fact that her salespeople were still as busy as ever making calls. When she began to get some qualitative data from her team and customers, she found that most client companies were just experimenting with digital placements once and then not buying again. So the salespeople couldn't build a book of repeat business that they could keep adding to. She then stepped back with her team and asked how they could measure the likelihood of repeat placements and found that "page views" (a measure of how many people actually looked at a digital ad) were a good predictor and something that the operations team (another part of the company) was already tracking. She then added page-view data to the regular metrics, which enabled her team to identify the probable repeat buyers and the types of ads that were most likely to succeed. Armed with this data, the team was able to increase sales significantly in the following months.

You will need to track a number of metrics simultaneously. That's why the outcome from answering these questions should be some form of dashboard or what Robert S. Kaplan and David Norton call the "balanced scorecard" in their HBR article "The Balanced Scorecard: Measures That Drive Performance." The basic idea of a balanced scorecard is to construct the right suite of measures to help you drive results for your team or organization—financial and operational, retrospective and prospective, quantitative and qualitative.

Having the right measures is only the beginning, however. You also must check in regularly with your team: that's where operational cadence comes in.

Set an effective operational review cadence

The thirty-day check-ins that Macia instituted for her rapid-results teams were critical forums for assessing progress and making midcourse corrections. But they were only part of the overall operational review cadence that Macia used to ensure that everyone's efforts added up to the results she expected. These regular reviews also included quarterly all-employee progress updates, weekly senior team meetings, regular one-on-ones with direct reports, and more. Despite the fact that much of her schedule was variable—filled with traveling to customers, meeting with her XL bosses, and handling unexpected events—the internal rhythm of meetings that she created allowed her and everyone on her team to keep the work on track.

Holding regular operational reviews creates a structure for knowing what results you are achieving and a regular forum for deciding how to systematically improve them or correct course. Your job as a leader is to establish this kind of cadence if it doesn't already exist, refine an existing cadence if it needs to be improved, or integrate the cadence for your team or division into that of the company. Think about how often you want to review progress, who else you need to involve, and what kinds of issues you want to highlight. Then put your operational reviews on the calendar, for you and for all the participants, and make sure that everyone honors these meetings as real commitments. You also should establish a regular agenda for the reviews, with some flexible space for unanticipated issues that might emerge.

For example, when Mark Benjamin was president and COO of NCR, he organized his review cadence around a weekly Monday morning virtual meeting with his team (located worldwide). As they went around the "room," each person gave updates on key performance goals and on issues that needed attention. "It's a major commitment to do this weekly," Benjamin admits, "but in a big company like ours, if we did it only once a month, there wouldn't be time to go deep enough on issues, and the lag time between updates would get people out of alignment with each other." Jane Kirkland, a senior vice president at State Street Corporation, also emphasizes the need to have regular reviews and disciplines. "Make sure you have a review process for everything that touches you," she advises leaders.

You can use the operational cadences to integrate your work in many areas of the business—and in many of the practice areas discussed in this book, from strategy and innovation to employee performance. In one classic example, Jack Welch of GE organized the various processes for his company in a rhythmic, interconnected sequence, which he depicted as a circular racetrack that he and his leadership team would regularly lap. The year began with a strategy discussion and update. Three months later, Welch and the team moved to business reviews raising issues out of the latest strategy. At midyear, there was course correction and talent check-ins, then more business reviews and performance management. By the end of the year, fresh issues and objectives set up the next year's strategy refresh. As the company kept going around the track, everyone involved shared learning and discussed and agreed on improvements to keep raising the collective performance and impact of GE. Based on this corporate cadence, each business unit and subunit throughout the company created cadences that matched and supported the overall rhythm.

Consider some of your team's own processes: can they be more tightly linked, with the learnings and decisions of each feeding directly into the next? If so, as your unit goes around the track, more and more managers and leaders will practice and learn about vision, strategy making, people recruitment and development, sustainable growth, and so on. And if you are not the CEO and don't control the enterprise cadence, think about how you integrate the cadence of your team into the broader framework. When do you need to prepare for reviews with your bosses, and how do you become confident that everyone is ready?

Lead candid dialogue at operational reviews

As a leader, you can't just set up reviews at which your team reports on metrics and results: you must use those meetings as opportunities to push on every aspect of your team's work—often brutally. By having regular, aggressively candid dialogues with your team about the business, you'll be able to quickly respond to performance misses and determine quickly what to do about barriers, problems, and opportunities that inevitably emerge.

In the XL case, we saw that Macia had candid discussions with her business leaders and direct reports. She extended that behavior to her reviews with project teams and on overall performance indicators, with the intention of modeling this candid dialogue so that it would become part of what had been an overly polite culture.

Unfortunately, encouraging and modeling this kind of dialogue can be difficult. You must avoid letting the candor lead to blaming, cover-ups, or distortion. To address any challenges standing in the way of delivering results, your team must confront the realities of the organization, not an airbrushed ideal.

To make your reviews fruitful, your questions should be tough and direct, but always clearly in the spirit of accelerating progress, illuminating unconscious assumptions, and solving problems. That way you'll not only advance the work, but build relationships and help the people involved learn and develop. Avoid becoming the leader who (perhaps out of their own insecurity) asks review questions only to prove that they are the smartest one in the room or to make someone squirm. Asking questions well should actually have the opposite result: many of the best leaders we've seen have an uncanny ability to engage in Socratic dialogue that helps people reach their own conclusions about what can be done to improve a plan or project or operation, which, of course, leads to much more ownership and learning.

When in an operational review, first ask probing questions about the team's or individual's current results, plans, and projects. What's working well? Where are you struggling and why? Has anything surprised you so far? Where do you need help, guidance, fresh ideas, or resources? Asking these questions not only teases out what's really happening and what needs to be done, but also gives you insight into your people.

Terra Firma CEO Andrew Géczy emphasized to us that sometimes his questions force his people to think about the business differently. For example, in his previous role at ANZ bank, his people served thirty-five markets with many products, and he found that reviews were filled with "big spreadsheets that didn't address the issues." He asked his operations leaders instead to answer a few simple questions on one page: How hot is the transaction engine running? What is our cost per transaction? What is our aspiration for cost in three years? Over time, those questions converted ANZ's thinking about its operating platform and put the organization on a path to delivering products to clients much more efficiently.

Don't stop with just a review of the business unit itself, though. Move on to questions about the broader context in which your team operates. One of a leader's most critical tasks is to help everyone connect their projects, results, and measures with the work of others so that they don't look at each individual issue or problem in isolation (remember the "team of teams" discussion in chapter 3). Otherwise, the individuals on your team will not recognize how their work might affect other projects or operations, or how to prioritize various initiatives. Only the leader—who must think about the connections with these groups all the time—can spur this kind of thinking.

For example, a few years ago, one of us was working with the senior leadership team of a major hospital network. Its regular reviews included updates about all of the organization's individual projects related to operating results, patient outcomes, technology introductions, and other critical shifts in the health-care landscape. But there were so many of these updates in each review that it was hard for anyone involved to tell which projects were most critical and where to designate the most resources. The team was so deep into the weeds that it had lost sight of the garden.

After several months of this, the president asked the team to create a diagram of all the projects included in the review and how they mapped against the organization's strategic priorities. This stark question forced the team to put the projects into context, and it was quickly apparent that many of the initiatives didn't advance the overall strategy. The president's question also encouraged the team to see just how little sequencing or sense of prioritization it had assigned to these efforts. Because everything was deemed important and had to be done right away, everyone, particularly the top 100 managers of the hospital network, was stretched thin and struggled to bring almost anything to completion. By asking these context questions, the president forced the leadership team to prioritize and streamline its efforts, which allowed it to better focus on the most important efforts to deliver results.

Of course, not every question you ask in a review will be a game changer. But if you have the courage to challenge assumptions and put initiatives in context, chances are that some of them will indeed make a difference, sometimes in surprising ways. And if you avoid asking tough questions, you'll start simply making assumptions about why projects may be off course or results different than expected. And when those assumptions are wrong, you'll create all sorts of dysfunctional patterns. In a financial services firm, for example, a major product upgrade was delayed for months because the product and IT managers had different assumptions about what was to be delivered by when, and kept blaming each other for delays. It took a senior sponsor finally stepping in to help them ask each other the right questions. Then they were able to come up with a plan that satisfied both and quickly produced incremental revenue for the product.

The leadership difference in achieving results

In summary, improving your organization's business results doesn't happen by itself or by random chance, and a focus on those results is not a onetime set of activities. It takes hard work and courage and, most importantly, has to be done again and again to eventually create a culture of high performance (see the box "Culture and results"). Without your leadership, people will rest on their laurels, avoid dealing with difficult barriers, use available measures instead of the right ones, and not confront each other about the reality of how they are doing. So driving for significant results is a never-ending process, and it's up to you to make it happen. That's what it means to be a leader.

Culture and results

Most leaders want their organizations to have a high-performance culture. This means that the drive for results and improvement is an ongoing norm, not a onetime event; that delivering on goals and commitments is expected; and that people at all levels understand that achieving results is a key criterion for personal success.

This kind of culture doesn't take root or flourish unless leaders intentionally move their teams in this direction through the steps we've described in this chapter and reinforce them repeatedly. As we saw from the XL case, Seraina Macia didn't inherit a high-performance culture, but had to create one by challenging her people, making them accountable for delivering, and putting mechanisms in place to continually hold their feet to the fire. Even then, it took Macia three years before the high-performance culture was firmly established.

(continued)

In their HBR article "Three Steps to a High-Performance Culture," Carolyn Dewar and Scott Keller describe a similar process at ANZ bank that also took several years. In their situation, executives took three key steps to change the culture that are similar to those we outlined in chapter 3. First, the ANZ executives explicitly stated what they wanted the high-performance culture to look like—that it would be characterized by alignment around vision, execution of goals, and continuous improvement beyond competitors' performance levels. They also created metrics to gauge progress on all three of these imperatives. Second, ANZ focused on a few key cultural attributes (such as customer focus) to reinforce every twelve to eighteen months instead of trying to change everything. And finally, ANZ integrated work on cultural issues into its business initiatives instead of dealing with them separately. The result of all this work was a significant rise in productivity per employee and other key performance metrics—all of which were sustained for ten years.

Think about your own team or department. To what extent is a high-performance culture already in place? If it is, what steps can you take to reinforce and sustain it? And if not, what can you do to move your culture in the direction of high performance?

Questions to consider

- **Stretch goals.** What goals could your team reach for that would make your customers and your senior leaders take notice? How high can you raise the bar?

- **Accountability.** What consequences have you set if members of your team do not achieve their goals? Do they truly feel like they *must* achieve the goals you set for them?

- **Reducing complexity.** How can you make it easier for people on your team to get things done? Can you run interference for them with other groups in your organization so that they can concentrate on what they need to do?

- **Building capability and confidence.** What 100-day projects can you create as good opportunities for people to learn about how to get results on a small scale first, even while achieving your team's biggest goals?

- **Metrics.** Do you have a clear and concise dashboard that tells you and your team how you are doing against your most critical goals? Do you have the right real-time measures for tracking progress and leading indicators that can help you make fast and nimble decisions?

- **Operational cadence.** Have you created a regular rhythm and discipline for reviewing progress with individuals and teams that report to you?

- **Review candor.** Are you satisfied with the candor of your team's reviews? Are you and others constructively challenging how things are done and then working together to solve problems and make improvements?

5.

Innovating for the Future

The enterprise that does not innovate ages and declines. And in a period of rapid change such as the present, the decline will be fast.

—Peter Drucker

Throughout this book we've offered ways for you as a leader to look ahead: whether you're setting a vision, crafting a competitive strategy, developing your team, or demanding better results, you are constantly pushing your team, unit, or organization into the future. In this chapter, we'll focus on how to establish the mechanisms and culture of innovation that increase the chances for growth and sustained performance over time.

Organizations that sustain their success consistently over the long term can be hard to find. Consider the experience of the Ford Motor Company. The iconic company struggled with years of red ink until the early 1990s, when its management revitalized product development, reawakened the organization's deeper purpose, and produced what Collins and Porras described in *Built to Last* as "a remarkable turnaround." Twenty years later, though, the company was again verging on bankruptcy due to structural cost disadvantages, slow reactions to market shifts, and a general lack of innovation. Then in 2008, it was rescued and transformed once more by CEO Alan Mulally, emerging as one of the world's most profitable car companies. Three years later, after Mulally's departure, more struggles ensued as Ford's profits and share price began to flatten. In 2016, the board fired the successor CEO, fearing the company was not positioning itself to survive in an industry being revolutionized by self-driving and electric vehicles.

Ford has managed to survive through these up and downs, but many companies don't. The average life span of an S&P 500 company has decreased from sixty-plus years in the 1950s to around seventeen years now. In his HBR article "The Scary Truth about Corporate Survival," Vijay Govindarajan reported on research at Dartmouth that looked at the longevity of almost 30,000 companies listed on US stock markets from 1960 to 2009 and found that companies that were listed before 1970 had a 92 percent chance of surviving the next five years, whereas companies that were listed from 2000 to 2009 had only 63 percent. According to the Small Business Administration, only 50 percent of small businesses last five years, and only 33 percent make it to a tenth anniversary. Most researchers say that nonprofits fail at about the same rate. Similarly, according to research by Boston investment firm Cambridge Associates, data suggests that 60 percent to 80 percent of all startups fail after five years, a rate somewhat higher than that of small businesses.

So why is sustained business success so ephemeral for most companies and many leaders? Every rise-fall-rebirth-fall-again story has its own particulars, but in the end, there are always two villains in the plot.

The first is external: even after a company has successfully transformed itself, markets will continue to shift, often suddenly; new technologies will emerge; and global economic shocks will periodically rock the system. When Mulally was heroically saving Ford, who could have predicted that within a few years, the company would see the explosive success of Tesla, the proliferation of ride-sharing transportation, or the accelerating progress of self-driving cars?

The second villain is internal: success breeds complacency, inward focus, and even arrogance. As your unit or company keeps winning, belief in the status quo hardens: "if we've done something well, there's no need to change." And that belief is only strengthened by cheerleaders—short-term investors, stock market analysts, exuberant customers—who keep urging you to do more of the same and not take bold moves that might rock the boat. Boston Consulting Group president and CEO Richard Lesser observed to us that most CEOs get trapped by their own success. They get accolades for a successful transformation or improved results, but then they aren't willing to take a hammer to what they have created and to transform it again to get to the next level. "In some ways you have to be able to start all over again periodically," he advises. "But you also have to instill that mindset into the organization so that there's always a healthy dissatisfaction with the status quo."

Overcoming these challenges is critical, whether you are heading a large enterprise, launching a startup, or leading a part of a bigger company. Sustaining your business into the future is a vital component of achieving impact. And for rising leaders, there's no better way to build the innovation skills and mindset you'll need at higher levels of an organization than to practice them hands on. You'll be able to make your mistakes and learn from those at smaller scale. And indeed, opportunities for innovation exist at all levels. If you're now heading a company division, a business unit, or even a small team, you need to understand how that team contributes to the overall organizational portfolio of today's cash and tomorrow's reinvention. And you need to be able to sustain your own part of the business into the future as well.

This is particularly true because a great deal of corporate innovation is bottom-up—it's not simply directed by a CEO or invented by an R&D department. Frontline leaders working closely with customers, suppliers, or other partners are exposed daily to different needs and opportunities in the market, new approaches to working, and insights about competitors, new technologies, and business-changing trends. Embrace these relationships for what they can teach you about the future of the business you lead now, as well as the broader organization that you may lead in the future.

Also, innovation exploration is not just for customer-facing managers. If you're leading a corporate function—finance, legal, technology, human resources, and so on—seek out opportunities to revolutionize processes or restructure costs for your group. Whatever your leadership level or role, try to learn something that may catch the eye of more senior managers and perhaps become a showcase for next year's broader corporate strategy.

There are four specific elements of this practice of actively championing future-focused innovation:

- **Balancing the present and future:** creating bandwidth to focus on the future while still maintaining high performance in day-to-day operations

- **Getting ready for the future:** developing the mindset, the funding, and the market intelligence to invest wisely in future-oriented areas of the business

- **Shaping the future:** driving the innovation, experimenting, and learning to move your organization into new territory

- **Building a future-focused culture:** infusing your organization with the skills, beliefs, and values to innovate well and to keep innovating and reshaping itself over and over again

As with all of the practices in this book, we do not mean that the steps we describe in these areas constitute a linear formula, but rather starting points for your own journey toward creating a sustaining enterprise. To give you a sense of what this means in practice, let's look at the experience of Jim Smith, CEO of Thomson Reuters, a leading provider of news, technology, intelligence, and expertise to finance, law, and other professional industries.

Building sustaining success at Thomson Reuters

When Jim Smith was promoted to CEO of Thomson Reuters in January 2012, he took the reins of a $13 billon global news and information powerhouse whose businesses included the Reuters news service; the world's largest publishing company and information resource for the legal profession; a Financial & Risk business that provided terminals and data feeds for major banking and trading institutions; a unit that served as the primary source of legal, regulatory, and compliance information for the tax and accounting profession; and an Intellectual Property and Science business that helped universities and researchers track and search scientific findings and patents.

Smith's most urgent challenge was to fix the Financial & Risk business, which was by far the largest in the company and had been losing share in a shrinking market for five consecutive years. The recession and financial crisis of the previous years had decreased demand for the terminals that were the bread and butter of the division's revenue. In his first year, Smith spent a significant portion of his time working with the Financial & Risk leaders on investments and strategies to turn the business around and achieve maximum sustainable growth and shareholder value.

In addition to his focus on the Financial & Risk unit, Smith spent time with the other business units to review their financial performance, growth plans, and resource requests. He also visited dozens of customers around the world, both to strengthen their relationship with Thomson Reuters and to better understand their challenges.

Early into the job, Smith concluded that he would need to change the way Thomson Reuters was managed—from a portfolio of individual operating companies into a far more integrated, less complex, and higher-growth enterprise. The organization had been built over more than a century through acquisitions, divestitures, combinations, and spinoffs (including 300 acquisitions in the previous ten years), and each of these structural changes brought different practices, systems, and ways of working. As a result, the company was overly complex, expenses were duplicated, processes were fragmented, technology was not being leveraged, leaders of the different businesses weren't learning or benefiting sufficiently from each other, and large enterprise customers needed multiple touch points and contracts to work with the company. Furthermore, this complexity made it more difficult to deliver the full breadth and depth of Thomson Reuters' capabilities across customer segments and diverted resources away from developing the technology and products of the future.

To address these issues, Smith set out to create an integrated, customer-focused enterprise that could take advantage of its scale and fuel its growth more through organic innovation than acquisitions—a transformation that would take a number of years.

During 2012, he began laying the groundwork for this transformation. He engineered the sale of a health-care business and some smaller businesses because they would not be key contributors to future growth. At the same time, he and his team approved and completed a number of small technology acquisitions to complement their existing digital platforms, such as an online brand protection company and a provider of electronic foreign exchange trading solutions.

While these steps helped sharpen the company's focus on its core businesses, they didn't directly move Thomson Reuters toward greater integration or organic growth. To do that, Smith concluded, he first needed managers to start tackling the organization's complexity.

During 2012, Smith's chief financial officer had found forty-two different billing systems that he consolidated into one. Aiming to replicate this effort, Smith made simplification and standardization a major priority for the company beginning in 2013. He added the newly created position of Chief Transformation Officer to his executive committee, a function that would eventually oversee nearly a third of the company's spend and head count, and publicly committed to investors that the company would reduce complexity-related expenses by $400 million by the end of 2017.

As the Financial & Risk division stabilized, Smith turned more of his attention toward the longer-term transformation of the company. As part of this shift, he worked with his staff to streamline the corporate operating rhythm to reduce redundant meetings, rationalize his personal calendar, and make way for even more time with customers.

To kick-start organic growth, Smith launched a number of innovation initiatives, coordinated by a central innovation team, to build a more flexible, dynamic, and forward-thinking culture inside the firm. A small but early and important success story came in the form of the Catalyst Fund.

This fund, set up by the corporate center, awarded seed money to individuals or teams that wanted to pursue potentially breakthrough new ideas, either in the form of new offerings or improved processes. Anyone could submit an idea, and the most promising were put in front of a review board once a month, chaired by Smith himself. Those who passed the first round of reviews used their funding to build proofs of concept that they could test with customers and then iterate upon. The most promising ideas emerging from this process would then be more fully funded as new products and services. Smith also asked his leaders to designate "innovation champions" throughout the organization to be involved in cross-company innovation initiatives, introduced future-focused metrics into business reviews, and established communications avenues and a yearly workshop where organic innovation activities could be discussed, coordinated, and celebrated.

Smith accompanied the innovation program with a deliberate initiative to make the company's culture more creative and collaborative. All managers and leaders, starting with Smith's executive team, went through a workshop and follow-up discussions meant to create a common language and expectations for behavior, which then were reinforced in performance reviews and promotion decisions. Smith also came to grips with the fact that several of his senior business unit heads and functional leaders had not fully bought into the idea of an integrated operating company and were not truly collaborating with each other, so he replaced several of these blockers at the same time. This gave Smith a more collaborative team and sent a strong signal through the company that everyone should take the culture of innovation and collaboration seriously.

By the end of 2014, Smith's transformation was beginning to bear fruit. Higher customer satisfaction and employee retention ratings were paired with a significant improvement in year-over-year net sales. The Financial & Risk business recorded its first year of positive net sales since the recession. Areas of the business targeting faster growth opportunities saw 4 percent aggregate revenue growth. And the simplification program improved operating efficiency and was on track to reach its savings targets.

Smith's efforts to position the company for the future have not let up since then. In recent years, the company has established a network of innovation labs around the world from Cape Town, South Africa, to Waterloo, Canada, where the company's technologists can work side by side with customers, partners, and startups, rapidly prototyping solutions. The company also formed partnerships with blue-chip technology firms like SAP and IBM Watson to power its solutions. In late 2016, Smith announced the creation of a new flagship technology center housing up to 1,500 staff in Toronto to take advantage of the growing concentration of engineering and technical talent in Canada's Silicon Valley and moved his headquarters there to reinforce the commitment. One year after the announcement, the company has hired over 200 technologists and data scientists, and announced a more than $100 million investment in a permanent facility for the center. And in early 2018, as a result of the successful efforts to turn around the Financial & Risk business, Smith sold a fifty-five percent stake in it to the Blackstone Group for $17 billion, giving Thomson Reuters greater financial flexibility to transform even further into the future.

In the six years since Smith became CEO, Thomson Reuters has become a vastly different company, now focused, as Smith puts it, at the intersection between commerce and regulation. As such, Thomson Reuters strives to help businesses of all sizes—from solo practitioners to global corporations—find answers to their most pressing problems. Along the way, the company has become more focused, more profitable, faster growing, and on the list of most admired and most desirable firms to work for. And while no company's future is ever guaranteed, Thomson Reuter's future seems more promising than ever.

Balancing the present and future

One of the biggest challenges for leaders is maintaining the continued operation of the core business or of their unit while also looking ahead to avoid future threats and create opportunities for future growth. While it's easier to focus on one or the other, as a leader, you must do both, even if you are working in a midlevel role and are primarily responsible for generating cash or other near-term operational results. Whatever your role, if you give all your attention to your everyday core, you can get mired in details and miss longer-horizon threats and opportunities. But if you veer toward too many blue-sky ideas and make major investments in them, you will miss next quarter's numbers or neglect key customers, threatening the success and longevity of your unit, as well as your own career. Achieving this balance is in part a logistical matter of making time for you to focus on innovation and, in part, a conceptual question of how to balance current and future work throughout the organization.

Creating bandwidth to focus on the future

Freeing up your time from being totally absorbed in day-to-day activities is a critical part of getting ready for the future. A leader can easily be so focused on current challenges and problems that there is no time to think about the next quarter, much less the next decade—think of Stephen Covey's dictum that the urgent drives out the important. This is one of the most pernicious traps that leaders fall into and that reduces their ability to create a sustaining enterprise, because if you focus on the future too late, it's already here and you're behind the curve. So while all of the steps that we described in the "getting results" practice in chapter 4 are critical, doing them at the expense of time to deal with the future is counterproductive.

Consider, for example, Jim Smith's move to reshape Thomson Reuters's operating rhythm to free up more of his own time for thinking, planning, and connecting with customers. This kind of shift is necessary in companies of all sizes. Yaron Galai, the founder and CEO of digital media startup Outbrain, did the same thing when his company reached a significant threshold of growth, and he realized that he no longer had enough time to focus on both managing the current business and figuring out the next chapter. As a result, he brought in an experienced operational leader who had been on the board to serve as a co-CEO, which allowed him to focus on the future of the company.

Finding bandwidth is often about personal discipline as much as organizational cadence. That kind of discipline is necessary for good leaders at every level: for example, Jane Kirkland, senior vice president of State Street Corporation, is relentless about organizing her time to make sure she doesn't get buried in day-to-day activities: "I work off of a regular list of to-dos that I keep, but I always categorize them across different time horizons, aligned with the people I'm holding accountable for different tasks."

We often see leaders struggling to have the humility to admit that they can't do it all, as if that is a black mark on their leadership. Instead, we urge leaders that we work with to see that this is the very hallmark of strong leadership: recognizing how to apportion tasks, roles, and areas of ownership to others to create the highest levels of performance for the organization overall.

Taking a portfolio approach to innovation

When you move your unit or team toward a dual focus on current business results and future innovation, tensions and trade-offs are inevitable. As innovative opportunities emerge, when and how much do you start favoring them over existing operations? If certain core business initiatives are flattening out, when do you cut back on investment? If certain experiments don't work out, do you discard them or double-down with even greater commitment? And how do you prevent the new future from cannibalizing what you need to keep going today? These questions are the essence of the "innovator's dilemma" that Harvard Business School professor Clay Christensen highlighted in his book of the same name—where the success of innovation threatens the existing business and may result in trade-offs that stifle the innovation.

To manage this tension, consider the model of financial portfolio management: instead of putting all of your money in one place, you spread it around and create a diverse portfolio of different types of investments— stocks, bonds, small cap, large cap, domestic, international, and so on. You then manage the risk and return in the portfolio by adjusting the mix and amount of investments dynamically, since it is unlikely that all of them will rise or fall to the same degree simultaneously. We can apply this concept to innovation as well. Tuck School of Business professors Vijay Govindarajan and Chris Trimble, in their HBR article "The CEO's Role in Business Model Reinvention," describe their "three box" approach. They argue that leaders need to balance and then continue to rebalance their investments between what should be "preserved and improved" in their current business, what should be "destroyed" because it is underperforming or has little upside, and what should be "created for the future." Their research suggests that most leaders significantly overweight their focus and investment on preservation, and don't put enough thinking and resources behind what should be destroyed and created for the future.

The portfolio idea extends beyond simply balancing riskier, long-range projects with low-risk, near-term growth. Even within their more innovative projects, companies such as Google, Intuit, 3M, P&G, and Apple don't put all their eggs in one basket. Instead they create portfolios of innovation projects, including some core initiatives and also innovation of different types, technologies, and markets. The companies then actively manage these portfolios by allocating resources differentially, periodically killing some projects while doubling down on others. One of the reasons that companies struggle with innovation is that they don't manage the portfolio of projects with enough rigor or discipline, allowing poorly performing efforts to continue while starving those with more potential.

You can organize your innovation portfolio along a number of different axes. One way is to include projects with different time frames. As Robert Schaffer and Ron Ashkenas described in their book *Rapid Results: How 100-Day Projects Build the Capacity for Large-Scale Change,* adhesives maker Avery Dennison used a framework developed by McKinsey that separated projects by time horizons: horizon one projects were short-term innovations (less than two years) that would use existing proprietary technology; horizon two were medium-term innovations (two to five years) that required modifications of existing technology; and horizon three were longer-term (more than five years) breakthroughs that required significant new research and development. (You can find numerous examples of horizon charts online.) Plotting projects in this way revealed to then-CEO Philip Neal and then-president Dean Scarborough that the company's investments were too heavily weighted toward longer-term projects that wouldn't pay off for many years (even if they were successful). To decrease risk, Neal and Scarborough shifted much more focus to horizon one projects that could pay off in the short term and provide a basis for funding the longer-term and more speculative initiatives.

Another way to measure your innovation projects is by focus area. For example, Thomson Reuters categorizes its innovation projects in terms of whether they will affect operations, customer experience, or product offerings. In each of these buckets, it also looks at how close or far the projects are from the current core, which is another way of assessing the time frame and potential return on the innovation. The company's Senior Vice President of innovation Katherine Manuel then maps out the existing innovation projects and reviews them periodically with the corporate leadership team so that they can decide how to balance their investments and expectations. As she notes, "It's important to have a portfolio of experiments being run that impact all types of innovation and all areas of the company."

At TIAA, the leading provider of financial services for the academic, research, medical, cultural, and government fields, CEO Roger W. Ferguson Jr. considered the parts of the business that needed to be sustained, both of which needed to evolve when building his portfolio. He would frequently cite, for example, the importance of preserving the integrity of the company mission: "We were founded to ensure that teachers could retire with dignity. Providing a secure retirement remains our purpose, but we now serve millions of others working to serve society in the nonprofit sector, and we strive to deliver financial well-being throughout all stages of life." At the same time, Ferguson also emphasized that the new TIAA had to be simpler to continue meeting its customers' needs, so it had to let go of old ways of thinking. Part of that was a decision to rebrand the company to the shorter identifier "TIAA," moving away from its old name (the company had been TIAA-CREF: think of Govindarajan and Trimble's first box—preserve and improve). In line with its drive to simplify, TIAA took a fresh look at its existing processes; in one case, it was able to cut a fifteen-day process down to two-and-a-half days. The value to customers was clear: the change reduced the number of customer phone calls by hundreds of thousands (thus, Govindarajan's box two—letting go of things now getting in the way of the future). In step with the new identity, Ferguson also accelerated growth across the company's nonretirement businesses. To do that, Ferguson commissioned a number of strategic growth teams to problem-solve new opportunities and develop new offerings, most recently resulting in the acquisition of EverBank, which will allow TIAA to meet the financial needs of its customers in a comprehensive way for generations to come (box three—create). Juggling all of this together—with a portfolio mindset—was critical for Ferguson's success.

Taking stock of your project portfolio periodically, therefore, is a critical step for embracing the future and creating a sustaining enterprise.

Getting ready for the future

In addition to carving out time to focus on the future, you must also prepare for it in other ways. To innovate, you need resources and information about threats and opportunities to guide your idea generation and experimentation. You can develop both of these as part of your unit's or team's day-to-day work.

Build current surplus to fund the future

Investing in the future requires that you first generate cash from your current operations. We saw this in the Thomson Reuters case: Smith reduced costs through simplification and focused on the turnaround of the Financial & Risk business at the beginning of his tenure. In other words, tightening up your execution and improving margins of your existing business is a good place to start. That's what John Lundgren, CEO of Stanley Black & Decker, did to raise the funds to buy several other companies at the outset of its multiyear growth plan. And whatever the scale of your business—whether you run a small venture or a unit within a larger company—operating ever more efficiently puts money in the bank for future growth and investment. But let's also look at two other ways to create some surplus for longer-term bets: developing product and market extensions (adjacencies) to generate more revenue from current operations and selling off or stopping lower-performing business areas.

Incremental innovation through adjacencies

Incremental innovation based on your current offerings is a common—and often lower-risk—way to build investment cash. Consider the matrix of

FIGURE 5-1

Adjacency opportunities for growth

	Existing products and services	New products and services
New markets	Sell current offerings to new markets and customers.	Engage in breakthrough innovation that develops new products and services for new markets and customers.
Existing markets	Increase current business in market share and volume.	Sell product extensions and variations to existing markets and customers.

products and markets in figure 5-1. With this framework, you can ask your business leaders (or even team members) to identify existing products or services that you could potentially introduce into new markets, and existing markets that would benefit from extensions or variations on your existing products. These categories of incremental innovation (the two shaded areas on the matrix) are called adjacencies. At TIAA, selling existing products to new professional groups (such as hospital staff) was a market adjacency, while diversifying investment and retirement options for existing higher ed customers was an example of a product extension. At Thomson Reuters, a major adjacent opportunity was to sell existing products to new geographic markets around the world, so it created a global growth organization with the specific objective of doing that.

Divesting

Another way to free up cash and resources to invest in future opportunities is to sell off or close products, units, or parts of your business that don't create great returns today and are likely not part of the future business.

What's difficult about this is not identifying which areas are ready for the chopping block, but rather setting aside your and others' emotional investment in an area that was at one time important for the business (or in former days was its own pioneering breakthrough; once again, the problem of the innovator's dilemma). But when the time comes, making the break is critical, as a way of freeing up both funds and other resources and your own attention.

For example, when Satya Nadella became CEO of Microsoft in 2015, he sold off the company's failing acquisition of Nokia's mobile handset division, realizing that it was not going to catch Apple or Google in smart phones. The money from the sale helped support Nadella's future growth strategy of moving Microsoft into more applications and services and becoming a more major player in cloud-based computing. Similarly, Smith at Thomson Reuters sold a health-care business and later the larger Intellectual Property and Science business because they were no longer at the core of the enterprise growth strategy. He also sold a major stake in the Financial & Risk business as a further way to build capital for the future.

Scan the horizon for breakthrough innovation

As you generate the cash, you also must be continually considering how to invest it, based on both potential opportunities and threats on the horizon. Your work in setting a vision and a strategy should give you a sense of this, but even apart from those specific practices, your understanding of a bigger picture for your business can help you identify particular areas for innovation. While some of the areas might be in the adjacency boxes depicted in figure 5-1, others might be in the upper-right quadrant—so-called breakthrough innovation, depicted in figure 5-2. Let's consider that now.

So-called breakthrough innovation involves a bigger leap (and usually a bigger risk-return profile) toward the future. As a leader, you must expand your awareness of new and more ambitious possibilities. Do so by scanning externally for new technologies, emerging new social or economic paradigms, or cutting-edge ideas in other industries that you could adapt. Be bold and creative in your investigations: start by engaging with customers, partners, and industry experts to find out what they are see-

FIGURE 5-2

Breakthrough opportunities for growth

	Existing products and services	New products and services
New markets	Sell current offerings to new markets and customers.	Engage in breakthrough innovation that develops new products and services for new markets and customers.
Existing markets	Increase current business in market share and volume.	Sell product extensions and variations to existing markets and customers.

ing or developing for their businesses. For example, CEO of Chevron Mike Wirth meets regularly with economists and other specialists to understand long-term scenarios for the price of oil and the latest advances in renewable energy technology. He also keeps tabs on more speculative ideas, for example, how the rise of ride sharing and electric cars could alter energy retailing. CEO of Bumble Bee Seafoods Chris Lischewski has participated in a futurist university program to better understand how broader social and economic trends among young consumers might open up future opportunities for marketing seafood.

Depending on your field, scanning could also include reading specialized research, talking to influencers in your field, or making benchmarking visits to noncompetitive visionary companies willing to share how the latest technology is changing their business. Car companies today meet with university researchers and automation boutiques to get ideas about self-driving and alternative transportation technologies. Other companies troop to Google, Facebook, and Amazon to learn about trends in robotics, artificial intelligence, and virtual reality, probing for implications for their own next generation of products. Many companies are also investing in mining big data of public and consumer information to analyze trends and opportunities in customer behavior.

While much of this work requires you to look outward, don't neglect your own backyard. Talking to people throughout your unit or organization—especially those on the front lines—will help you discover weak and not-so-weak signals about where your market is headed. Your best salespeople will be aware of changing customer tastes and competitors' innovations, and your engineers or product people often have strong relationships with other insightful industry practitioners. Leading innovation means listening to your own people as much as guiding them on what to do.

It can be exciting to identify possible opportunities, but you need to be clear-eyed about the threats as well. Anne Mulcahy's turnaround of Xerox, for example, was partly fueled by her personal understanding of how competitors were leapfrogging the company's products and services with a superior value proposition, an understanding she drew from her days working in sales. Paula Kerger's multiplatform strategy for children's programming was developed partly because she realized how much digital educational content was now encroaching on broadcast viewership and the traditional business model of PBS. At TIAA, the business model threat came into focus for Ferguson when he analyzed the company's longer-term payout viability and realized that baby-boomer retirements could impact the long-term financial strength of the company.

As a leader, you can never become complacent or let your team become satisfied. By incorporating this kind of scanning into your daily work, you'll prime your team or unit to take advantage of opportunities and avoid threats—right away.

Shaping the future

How do you act on the opportunities and threats you've identified in your operating environment, once you have the resources in place to do so?

Innovation should not be just a random exercise in brainstorming and trying things, but an intentional approach to evolving the company toward a significantly new value proposition and relationship with customers, while also sharpening and learning more about the value proposition along the way.

At Thomson Reuters, the new Catalyst Fund encouraged managers to pursue systematic and disciplined organic innovation through incremental steps and ongoing learning from customers. To secure the money, teams filled out a simple two-page application, describing the idea, its potential payoff, what would be needed to make it happen, and how the initial funds would be used. Applications were screened first by innovation champions and then a Catalyst Fund panel—a sort of corporate shark tank—composed of Smith and several members of the executive team. The committee met monthly, both to decide on these new applications and to see the output of projects in which it had previously invested.

Once the innovation leaders began to get traction in their own businesses and functions, and the bosses understood that innovation was now part of their jobs, ideas and innovation opportunities started to emerge from all corners of the organization. For example, Adam Quinones, a manager in the Financial & Risk business, used the Catalyst Fund process to propose and then develop an app to enable mortgage-related document and data validation, risk and liquidity assessment, and customer data and document storage for the commercial real estate industry. After building a prototype, Quinones organized a forum for potential customers to test the product. Based on the customers' feedback and enthusiasm, Quinones was able to refine the product and begin to sell it, creating real value to customers and a supercharged revenue stream for the company.

Every team's and company's situation is different, and there is no one-size-fits-all approach for transforming innovative ideas into breakthrough growth engines. You will need to develop your own process. But three ways of thinking about innovation should inform it: getting a jump on disruptive innovation, leveraging the lean startup approach, and embracing failure in the service of learning.

Disruptive innovation

Harvard Business School professor Clay Christensen first coined the term "disruptive innovation." As he describes, disruptive innovation is a process by which a smaller competitor quietly develops a new business model and, in so doing, suddenly shifts the competitive dynamics of an entire industry and its well-established companies. A classic example is Netflix's transformation of the video rental industry, undercutting Blockbuster's business by using the US mail to deliver DVDs straight to customers, with no due dates, late fees, or crippling real estate costs. Netflix then disrupted the movie and broadcast television industry by offering on-demand content for a subscription fee.

In contrast, Christensen defines "sustaining innovation" as continual experimentation to improve and refine an existing business model. While sustaining innovation can provide substantial incremental growth, mastering disruptive innovation means that incumbent companies are more prepared for unanticipated threats and better able to transform as technologies and new ideas around them develop. Mastering disruptive innovation also can help startups launch themselves into established markets.

As a leader in an established company, you need to realize that unusual and often unseen competitors can disrupt your business at any time. If you are in a startup and can find the right business model, you can be one of those disruptors. Particularly because of the enabling aspects of digital infrastructure, you often don't need large amounts of capital to enter established markets, but can instead find ways to pick off customers at the margins. As more and more free information becomes "good enough," Thomson Reuters, for example, uses its innovation mechanisms to identify specific market needs that it can meet with slices of professional data that come available directly or through partnerships with startups.

If you run an established company or division, one way to prevent your own business model from being disrupted is to develop disruptive ideas yourself. In their HBR article "Meeting the Challenge of Disruptive Change," Christensen and Michael Overdorf explain that doing this is usually difficult because your resources, processes, and decisions about priorities and investments are geared to the existing business and won't accommodate or support an idea that doesn't fit the current framework. To overcome that and avoid the rejection of disruptive ideas out of hand, you can set up a special team of dedicated resources, separate from the existing business processes and pressures, to focus on the new idea. For example, several years ago, a large pharmaceutical company that one of us worked with set up a small full-time team, led by a senior executive, to explore the development of an industrywide data analytics business that could mine actionable insights about drug development from clinical trial data, prescription sales, clinical tests, and genomic mapping. Although the team wasn't able to turn this idea into a stand-alone functioning business, many of the tools and approaches that it developed were incorporated into the core business. Another example of this approach is a technology unit at AIG called Blackboard Insurance, run by Seraina Macia (whom we met in chapter 4 when she was CEO of the XL North American P&C business). Blackboard is a dedicated team, separate from mainstream AIG, focused on disrupting insurance underwriting by incorporating artificial intelligence and data algorithms into the process.

If a disruptive idea does emerge from a dedicated team, and if it can't be developed further within the confines of the current business, then you can create a completely separate entity to bring it to market. The classic example is the way IBM developed its personal computer business in the 1980s (sold to Lenovo in 2005) by setting up a skunk works unit in a separate location with its own resources and without the inhibiting strictures and rules of the parent company that was at the time so beholden to selling mainframe computers. This kind of freedom allowed the IBM team to do whatever it needed to be successful, such as hiring and paying people differently, sourcing parts in new ways, creating new partnerships, and setting up separate sales channels. Another example was former CEO Jeff Immelt's structure for GE's software business, focused on the internet of things, which he created as a semiseparate entity located away from the core businesses—once again creating a culture more geared to high-tech innovation than the company's standard industrial production.

In addition to setting up new, more independent entities, you also can spin off parts of your business as a way of separating the traditional core (with its sustaining innovations) from the more revolutionary areas that are more likely to create disruption. A recent example of this is Hewlett-Packard's split into HP Inc. and HP Enterprise. HP Inc. focuses on the core printer business, which has lower margins and innovates incrementally. HP Enterprise, on the other hand, focuses on creating value for large corporate and governmental customers by developing new technology platforms and computing approaches. By separating into two firms, each could develop processes and prioritization rules more suited to the type of innovation needed. (Two years later, HP Enterprise doubled down on the strategy, dividing itself again by spinning off the lower-margin IT services included in the original partition.)

Even if you don't go through a full process of disrupting your organization, engaging in a what-if thought exercise can be useful. For example, in 2001, Jack Welch issued a challenge to all of the GE businesses to "destroy your business.com." The challenge of this iconic CEO was for each business—big and small—to actively consider how an unforeseen competitor, perhaps a startup in a garage, could compete and win against each established GE business. This was an eye-opener for many GE executives and leaders, who had become somewhat complacent in thinking that the only threats to their businesses would come from large competitors. As a result, many of them began to experiment with the disruptive ideas themselves— for example, the use of remote sensors for customer service, or mechanisms for self-service sales.

Corporate venturing and partnering

Another way to deal with potentially disruptive competitors is "don't beat 'em, join 'em" (or have them join you). Many large companies, for example, have venture or acquisition teams that actively look for startups, path-breaking tech entrepreneurs, and university partners, and then invest in them, buy them, or partner with them as they develop their innovations and business models. We described how Thomson Reuters built these kinds of partnerships earlier in this chapter.

To make corporate venturing or acquisition work a source of future growth, leaders need to guide each investment so it prioritizes intelligence gathering and learning over immediate operating returns, though financial rewards may also accrue over time. Nike, for example, developed a venture-investing group that specifically looked for new technologies, startups, or small companies that were pioneering new approaches to sustainable (environmentally sound) manufacturing. When it found a company that was attractive, it made a small, minority investment that allowed it to have a seat on the board (or advisory group) and learn about the technology. Once the technology matured, so that it was worthy of incorporation into Nike's manufacturing approach, it would either cut a licensing or partnership deal with the company or buy it outright. You might not be in a position to create a corporate venture investment group or make acquisitions, but you should always be looking for startups and new technologies that might have an impact on your business. And if you are leading a startup, you can identify corporate venture or acquisition groups that might be worth approaching too.

Lean innovation

A second approach to innovation that is important for building a sustainable enterprise is the "lean startup" model described in Steve Blank's HBR article, "Why the Lean Start-Up Changes Everything," which we first referenced in our discussion of strategy. While Christensen's approach focuses on the outside threat of disruption, the lean approach focuses on the process for advancing, changing, or discarding innovative ideas: it is an approach for systematically testing and developing a new business model for a new feature, product, startup, or unit. It may be part of developing a new strategy, simply exploring and refining sources of potential innovation, or both.

The core of the approach is rapid experimentation with real customers. Blank observes that creating detailed theoretical business plans for a new venture is often a waste, since those plans usually reflect a number of untested and usually false assumptions about customer behavior and desires. It's better to spend your time rigorously and quickly testing those assumptions. Do this by actually talking to potential customers—dozens of them—throughout the process of creating your new product or venture. As a result of these customer development dialogues, your people can then confirm the idea, pivot to a better idea, reconfigure it in some way, or drop it altogether. This means that nice and interesting innovation ideas or even sexy new technologies don't end up wasting time and resources, but can "fail fast." It also means that when you launch new enterprises, the chances of success are much higher, because you based them on confirmed principles. We saw this approach in the mortgage servicing innovation app at Thomson Reuters and in the exploration of the combined digital and broadcast approach in the development of the PBS KIDS 24/7 channel (discussed in chapter 2).

Leaders of teams and organizations are often the ones with the most outside view, but the lean methodology requires everyone in the process to connect to potential customers and their understanding of the product. It's easy to sit around and congratulate everyone on their innovative ideas or vote among yourselves about which are most promising. Real innovation and sustaining value, however, derive only from customers that are willing to buy your product or utilize your service, and engaging them up front means that you know you are building something they are interested in.

For example, Avery Dennison, as part of its drive to create sustainable growth through innovation, launched several innovation teams as a pilot. Each team took an idea that had been developed within the company and then went out to potential customers to reshape it and make it more viable. The challenge to each team was to get some first sales results within 100 days, and to do that, they had to find real customers. One team, for example, took a foil product used in heating, ventilating, and air-conditioning applications and reconfigured it into an adhesive tape by talking with potential customers and then partnering with a major home improvement company. In so doing, it had the first sales in the prescribed 100 days and then expanded the product from there. Based on this and other pilots, Avery eventually launched dozens of teams, involving hundreds of people, and generated millions of dollars in new revenue—a tangible path toward shaping the future.

Encourage controlled failure

Whatever your approach to innovation, you and your organization must be willing to learn from failure. Failure is a necessary component of learning. If organizations don't sometimes try things that are risky and have a higher than usual chance of failure, they can never create new forms of value. However, most organizations (and, in fact, most people) avoid taking on risk because they don't want to fail or suffer the public shame of doing so. We've all been taught that failure is bad. And it certainly can have career consequences or financial implications. But as you build your innovation process, you must build it in such a way that it allows failures to happen, in controlled ways, and to leverage what those failures can teach you.

As an example, one of Thomson Reuters's innovation champions, Bob Schukai, was an early tester of Google Glass (a device developed to display hands-free information on the lenses). Schukai and his team developed an application that would allow law enforcement officers to rapidly access information on their glasses at traffic stops. When Google stopped its Glass project, the application died with it. But its development had helped Thomson Reuters better understand information needs in the public sector, gain familiarity with public databases, and address privacy and safety concerns that it could use in various other projects. As innovation leader Manuel reflects, "The Google Glass project may not have ended with a multimillion-dollar revenue stream for us, but it sent a powerful message to all of our employees that innovation is alive and well."

To encourage failure in a controlled way, find opportunities for lean testing of initiatives like those described, in which concepts and assumptions are tested incrementally and thus with less risk. We've also seen this in action in the results practice we described in chapter 4, in the rapid experimentation exercises Seraina Macia led to get her team to reach the high goals she had set. Other experiments can be even more lightweight—in a "painted door" test, for example, a company advertises a product on the web to measure customer interest before it actually builds it. Interested users who click on the image get a message asking for their email so they can be notified when the product is ready or if they want to participate in further product testing. But if clicks on the ad are low, then the company doesn't invest further, which saves time and money, and the failure then frees up space for testing the next new idea quickly and frugally. Intuit uses this approach frequently as a way of quickly learning whether a new product or feature will have traction with customers or not.

Another way to encourage risk taking, failure, and learning is to set up a separate unit for developing a new business, product, or service, similar to what we discussed as part of disruptive innovation. In his HBR article "Planned Opportunism," Vijay Govindarajan stresses that this kind of "new-co" operates with a different set of metrics and expectations so that it can operate more freely and not have to hit the targets that would ordinarily apply and might stifle risk taking in the "core-co." He describes IBM's use of "emerging business opportunity" units that can test embryonic business ideas without the usual requirements to return capital, achieve revenues, and so on. This doesn't mean that the teams in these units don't have goals, but that the goals are more appropriate to a nascent idea than to an established business. You can also set up an incubator within your company to serve this function.

How to learn from failure

Processes for encouraging failure are one thing; learning from it is another. In their HBR article "Increase Your Return on Failure," Julian Birkinshaw and Martine Haas suggest three steps to make sure that you use your mistakes to grow: learn from every failure, share the lessons, and identify patterns. The after-action review (AAR) process originally developed in the military is a structured and systematic way of doing this. In their HBR article "Learning in the Thick of It," Marilyn Darling, Charles Parry, and Joseph Moore explain that AAR consists of a series of meetings and discussions with participants in a project or innovation team to assess what worked or what did not, what assumptions were used, and what should be done differently to improve either the current project or the next one. The outcome is not just a report, but also provides specific lessons linked to future actions, with clear accountability assigned for putting them into practice.

As an example, many years ago one of us worked with Johnson & Johnson's business development leaders to assess their process for integrating acquisitions, which was a key strategy for growth and innovation. After interviews with managers from a number of companies that had been brought into J&J (with varying degrees of success), several lessons emerged, such as the need for a full-time integration manager to be part of every acquisition, and for corporate functions to limit the number of requirements they placed on new acquisitions. These lessons and others were discussed with the CEO and his leadership team and then applied to the next large acquisition. Based on the after-action experience of that integration, the learnings were further adjusted so that J&J became increasingly skillful at integrating acquisitions.

Building a future-focused culture

Setting up a process and structure for innovation in your unit or team is one thing. But the process can never succeed if you don't also build a culture to match. An innovative culture is one in which your employees are (and you encourage them to be) intellectually curious, open to change, resilient, and flexible. It means that they actively learn new ways of working (and learning from failure). It means they are future oriented, thinking for the long term. And it means that they have an appreciation and capability for innovation itself.

These qualities are imperative for innovation because they enable managers and staff in the organization to embrace the future rather than resist it. But there is an added benefit. What happens when you're no longer leading that organization and can't personally steer it into the future? Building a culture centered around continuous innovation means that the organization is set up to succeed long after you are gone. Leaders after you will inherit an institutional capability and have a strong foundation upon which they can build. Research by McKinsey's Dom Barton and others suggests that when leaders build this kind of long-term thinking into the way the company does business, it creates significantly greater financial return, market capitalization, and job creation over the long term—and not by a little, but by a lot (see the HBR article by Barton and others, "The Data: Where Long-Termism Pays Off").

As we saw in chapter 3, shifting your organization's culture is not easy and depends on building the right leadership team, facilitating the right team interactions throughout the organization, giving tough feedback, fostering learning and development, and creating the right incentives. Let's examine what that looks like from an innovation perspective.

Developing a learning capability

The ability to learn rapidly is a critical capability for any organization committed to innovation. You can hire for this skill, but you also must develop your existing talent and put in place structures and mechanisms to foster the capability throughout.

As part of Thomson Reuter's transformation, Smith and his human resource team emphasized recruiting staff with technological, entrepreneurial, and problem-solving skills, and spent extra time coaching them to be successful in the emerging transformation. But he and his senior executives also coached other rising leaders in the organization who showed interest and ability to help reinvent the company, such as the innovation champions and the corporate innovation team. Smith made sure that individuals who showed interest and skill in innovation were involved in workshops, hackathons, and projects throughout the transformation process and would deliberately seed them in different initiatives across the organization. Leadership programs in the company also were aligned with the emerging future direction. And as the transformation advanced, Smith also made sure that human resources and performance management systems were updated and aligned with changes in the business. Smith's creation of the technology center in Toronto, which allows engineers and developers who are working on common topics, like artificial intelligence, to be co-located, was another way that Smith and his team strengthened the learning capability.

Boeing gives us another example of what it takes to build a culture of innovation. Before Jim McNerney retired as Boeing CEO in 2015, he realized that the company's continued success demanded that its people and partners approach problem solving and product development in new and different ways. McNerney worked with his successor Dennis Muilenburg, who became president in 2013, CEO in 2015, and chairman of the board in 2016, to identify the internal capabilities Boeing needed to compete and win in its second century. (The company began operating in 1916.)

To foster this new capability, senior business leader Pat Dolan was appointed to work with the businesses and with Human Resources to teach managers and engineers how to differentiate between incremental change and step-function change, and how to handle the latter more effectively. Dolan explained to us that for incremental changes, the company had plenty of subject matter experts who could develop solutions. But for challenges that hadn't been faced before, they didn't necessarily know how to approach them—there were no detailed plans to execute. "Instead," Dolan said, "we need to empower people to learn as fast as possible so that they can be successful. The key is not fast execution, but fast learning."

To develop his organization's learning skills, Dolan and his colleagues brought teams of Boeing people together for multiday workshops to tackle real, intractable problems that required substantial change. The outcome of each of these sessions was a "learning plan," rather than a detailed plan of what would be done. Dolan explained: "We keep it at a high level so they don't get lost in details too early. They have to figure out the path that they are going down first and not lock in too quickly." Once they had this learning plan, the teams were asked to return to their businesses—working with other functions, suppliers, and partners—and actually make progress against the problem. They then came back for another workshop several months later to reflect on what they accomplished and learned, and how they approached the problem differently.

Dolan believes that this process represents at least a four-year journey toward developing new capabilities and strengthening the company's culture. After all, the previous culture took 100 years to create. After several years, Dolan and his team have sponsored approximately forty of these workshops with an average of fifty people at each one—and with continued reinforcement from senior company leadership. As a result, nearly 2,000 key managers and engineers have begun learning how to address problems differently and with more flexibility, skills needed to help Boeing develop and inspire its people, innovate more quickly, and further grow its business.

Incentivizing innovation

In order for innovation to take root and become part of the culture, people on your team or in your organization have to feel that you will reward and recognize the pursuit and development of new ideas, and not dismiss or punish them. Doing this is more difficult than it might seem. For most ongoing enterprises, no matter whether large or small or for profit or nonprofit, incentives are inevitably weighted toward maintaining, servicing, and incrementally growing the current business. After all, you don't want people to sit around and daydream and doodle when there's work to be done. Some companies (e.g., 3M and Google) famously encourage employees to spend a certain percentage of their time working on speculative and innovative projects. But these are the exceptions. Most companies focus their people on what needs to get done today, while leaving innovation for the future to the R&D group or a few senior executives.

As part of the TIAA transformation, Ferguson knew that new ideas and innovation had to come from many parts of the company, not just from him. He encouraged new business exploration more widely with the creation of growth teams comprising people from different functions, tasking them with explicit objectives to pursue and develop new ideas. Ferguson also actively promoted people who exhibited the spirit of innovation, and he made a point of knocking down potential procedural and process blockers that were getting in the way of new ideas. Ferguson also communicated constantly about the firm's transformation and publicly recognized people who were at the forefront of TIAA's reinvention.

Thomson Reuters' Catalyst Fund exemplifies another kind of incentive mechanism that goes beyond just the promised seed money. Employees at all levels were energized not just by the cash, but by the promise of improving the business itself. Indeed, the internal publicity about the initial winners and the overall process triggered a steady flow of applications.

Over four years, nearly 100 ideas were funded, many of which have been put in the market and have given the overall fund a very healthy return on investment.

In addition, many of Thomson Reuters's innovation initiatives have helped make organic innovation part of the culture. Driven by an executive sponsor and a full-time innovation leader, these have included:

- Building innovation metrics such as number of ideas in each stage of the innovation pipeline, the overall participation level of employees by rank and location, and survey results on employees' sense that they can be innovative and receive recognition for their efforts

- Appointing "innovation champions" in every business. Each businesses and corporate function designated a senior high-potential manager to help implement programs and processes to achieve the new goals and metrics. In addition, the champions created a common terminology for and built an online Thomson Reuters network filled with resources that employees could use to educate themselves about the concepts and practices of innovation

- Orchestrating a communications campaign with blogs, articles, and video interviews with internal innovators and other employees' views on innovation

- Organizing enterprise innovation workshops, with representatives from all parts of the business, to identify and plan efforts that would drive new or existing products or process solutions across the company's platforms

- Launching an "operational innovation fund," similar to the Catalyst Fund, to encourage more creative back-end software development for operations centers

- Establishing Innovation Challenges to crowdsource solutions plaguing an area of the business or a customer group

- Supporting the innovation lab network, housed within the Technology organization, but leveraged across the entire company to consider emerging technologies and the art-of-the-possible to build solutions for the future

All these steps, directed by a senior-level innovation steering committee, were initiated as experiments to focus on learning, adjusting, and figuring out what would work over time and then were iteratively improved. For example, the innovation metrics were sharpened as the definitions of innovation evolved, and the experience of the first few innovation champions helped clarify criteria for selecting additional ones. Also, all these steps were carried out with as much transparency as possible, so that all Thomson Reuters employees not only would know what was happening, but could themselves contribute to the efforts along the way. In describing Thomson Reuters's goals, Katherine Manuel reflects: "Much of what we did was to democratize ideation and rapid experimentation and communicate successes and failures. Our aim was to create as many opportunities for employees, no matter what level they are, which business they reside in, or where across the globe they sit, to participate. We wanted all employees to associate making changes to improve what they do and how they do it as innovation: this is where innovation at scale can fundamentally shift the performance of a large organization."

As a result of all this work, after just a few years, organic growth through innovation has become well established as the norm at Thomson Reuters. The innovation network is one of the most visited sites on the company's intranet. Employees submit hundreds of ideas for consideration at the enterprise innovation workshops and challenges. Catalyst Fund projects are regularly prototyped, piloted, and then rolled out to customers. And the businesses have a robust portfolio of pioneering new ideas that are moving through their pipelines. So although there is still much to be done, and the jury is still out, clearly the company now has incentives in place to sustain an ongoing innovation culture.

Modeling innovative thinking

Your behavior as a leader sends strong signals about the kind of culture you are trying to create (as we discussed in chapter 3). Thus, to build innovation into your unit's or company's DNA, you and your leadership colleagues must personally demonstrate and exemplify it all the time. Ferguson at TIAA provides an illustrative case: throughout the corporate transformation of the business, this CEO did his best to model the behavior suited to future-seeking growth: displaying curiosity and excitement about new ideas while still respecting the importance of day-to-day business, showing genuine concern for others in his personal exchanges across the enterprise to build trust for learning, and serving on nonprofit boards, both to demonstrate his commitment to the values of service while also developing insights about the future from other organizations. He also encouraged his other senior leaders to do the same.

Similarly at Boeing, CEO Dennis Muilenburg regularly participates in candid, problem-solving dialogues with innovation workshop participants at the company's learning center in St. Louis, Missouri, and tries to think along with them as they tackle difficult business challenges. Muilenburg also insists that each innovation workshop team has a senior sponsor from the executive ranks who can challenge the team to think creatively and come up with innovative solutions. Their participation makes it clear to team members and others who hear about the teams that innovation is important for everyone.

The same is true at Thomson Reuters. At Catalyst Fund meetings, the company's leaders ask tough questions, encourage risk taking, and display the openness needed to foster creative thinking. In doing so, these senior executives model the importance of commercialization, signaling that "cool ideas" aren't embraced for their own sake, but must actually solve customer problems. While encouraging creative thinking, they still remind people at all levels that innovation is ultimately a means for delighting customers and growing the enterprise.

Sustainability is up to you

There is no magic formula for continuous reinvention and ensuring that your unit or company will be sustained for the long term. The innovator's dilemma is still alive and well and is not easy to overcome. But if you get ready for the future, manage a portfolio of innovation projects that helps shape the future, and embrace a culture that supports adaptability and change, you'll dramatically increase your chances of enduring success.

Wherever you sit in an organization, or whatever kind of organization you work in, adding future thinking and discovery to your job is also a stepping-stone for longer-term success. It will doubtless take you out of your comfort zone—there's nothing easier than simply focusing on tomorrow's deadlines—but it's a discomfort every great leader has learned to embrace.

Questions to Consider

- **Balancing your own time.** How much time do you spend focusing on getting things done today versus planning for the future? If your time is overly skewed toward the present, how can you create capacity for developing longer-term opportunities?

- **Scanning the environment.** What do you do to identify and keep track of potential threats and opportunities for your team, both inside and outside your organization?

- **Solidifying the core and building surplus.** Is your key existing business well managed? Is it creating some extra headroom to explore and pursue future-seeking opportunities?

- **Innovation portfolio.** Do you have a portfolio of innovative experiments—with different time frames and risk profiles—that can help you and your team shape the future?

- **Freeing up time for innovation.** Which of your team's activities can you divest or stop that will give you more time and resources for innovation?

- **Building capability to innovate.** Do your team members understand different types of innovation such as incremental adjacencies and disruptive and lean innovation? How can you educate them on these different approaches and give them opportunities to learn them through experience?

- **Failure and learning.** To what extent is it all right for people on your team to take risks and fail? What can you do to encourage the right kind of controlled risk taking and deliberate learning?

- **Culture for innovation.** What can you do to motivate your team members, individually and collectively, to continually look for new and better ways to conduct your business or contribute to your organization and customers? Can you give them time or seed money to shape new ideas? How well do you model a culture of innovation?

6.

Leading Yourself

Successful careers are not planned. They develop when people are prepared for opportunities because they know their strengths, their method of work, and their values.

—Peter Drucker

Because leadership creates significant impact through the work of others, we've devoted much of this book to what you need to do with and for your organization. That's not to say, though, that a focus on yourself is unimportant. Indeed, organizational impact ultimately rests with you, and if you are not equipped to handle it, success will be hard to find. To lead others successfully, you must also lead yourself.

In this chapter, we thus turn our outward focus inward, squarely at you, the developing leader, to help you build your own personal impact in your organization and in the world. As you progress in your career, what do you need to know about yourself to lead? How best to learn the things you need to know or practice the skills you need to master? What new opportunities should you accept? In what ways do you need to change and adapt to take more responsibility, while still remaining true to who you are? What relationships do you need to build? And how do you take care of yourself through it all? These are not onetime questions for you. Such challenges will evolve and become even more important as you step up to bigger and bigger roles throughout your career.

Successful leaders exhibit a wide range of skills and traits, and follow many different routes to developing themselves: there isn't one right way to guide yourself down the leadership path. In each section, we'll provide questions to ask yourself and to help you make the right decisions for your own personal journey. This practice involves four elements:

- **Knowing yourself:** the bedrock of leading yourself, understanding who you are and what you stand for, what you're good and not so good at, and how the world sees you

- **Growing yourself:** pursuing the most effective paths toward growth, especially those that help you learn by doing

- **Sharing yourself:** contributing your energy, knowledge, and skills to develop others

- **Taking care of yourself:** managing the physical and emotional aspects of your own welfare

Knowing yourself

The call to first and foremost "know yourself" is as old as Socrates. The philosopher's famous dictum remains as relevant as ever for leaders in today's organizations.

Knowing yourself is fundamental to forming a vision for your organization that reflects your own values and to giving the right priority to the work you care about. It allows you to understand and motivate others; your colleagues and associates will have an easier time following your lead when they sense that you know who you are. People want to understand the person they're signing up to work with, which is always easier to grasp when you're clear about that, too. Developing self-knowledge also means recognizing how you still need to grow to be more effective as a leader and that you'll know how to take care of yourself in your job, especially as you gain more responsibility and step up to ever more complex challenges.

But knowing yourself is legendarily difficult. We never see ourselves 100 percent objectively. Holding up the mirror can be painful because we too often imagine ourselves as what we want to be, not who we are. And achieving self-knowledge is even more difficult as you grow as a leader. As your responsibility and power increases, others will often tell you only what they think you want to hear. A former foundation executive provided us with his own small case study: "I never had the slightest hint that I was difficult to deal with until I resigned from my job and stopped giving out grants."

Knowing yourself requires persistent listening and reflection. You must keep probing for input and perspectives from others, using both formal and informal means. We discussed earlier in the book how developing people and operational performance requires a constant commitment to offering (often tough) feedback; you too need to commit yourself to receiving the same. That requires real humility, listening to criticism you may not want to hear, having the patience to reflect on it, and then summoning the courage to act on the right suggestions for how to improve.

Self-knowledge, like all forms of knowledge, best begins with questions. Ask yourself about three areas of self-knowledge:

- Your character

- Your personal style and habits

- Your knowledge and skills

Let's look at each in more detail.

Your character

What is your sense of purpose? What do you believe, hold true, and care about? What are you aiming at in your life overall? What are your aspirations? What inner strength do you call upon to win at what you do and to be resilient in the face of challenges?

Your answers will help you define your character: the more personal, intangible, and ethically oriented aspects that define who you are. Character tends to form through childhood and early adulthood, and many aspects of it will remain constant throughout your life. But people do change and evolve over time and grow in their self-understanding, which may reshape certain aspects of what they believe and care about. As a leader, you'll find it helpful to keep reflecting on the values and beliefs that are your inner North Star, the core that guides your decisions and actions as a member of human society and that your followers will use in committing themselves to your leadership.

Consider more deeply the following aspects of character in yourself.

Purpose

Why do you do what you do? What impact do you want to have on the world?

Your deeply held personal beliefs will directly inform and shape the work you do with your organization. As we saw in chapter 1, when leaders develop a vision, it must honor the broader purpose of the organization itself, and they'll be most effective when their personal sense of purpose aligns with that. For example, PBS president Paula Kerger has had a life-long commitment to educating and improving American society through media. She's been a revered leader at PBS because she so authentically aligns and believes in the mission of the system, as seen in her support of a new children's channel strategy. Stanley McChrystal, born into a family tradition of military service, inspired followers far and wide with his patriotic purpose of developing a new approach to countering the terrorism of Al Qaeda in Iraq.

Your purpose may be constant, or it may evolve over your working life. After years in different companies, John Lundgren became CEO of Stanley Black & Decker at the end of his career because of his personal desire to turn around an iconic brand headquartered in New England where he grew up.

Values

What are the principles and standards you aim to follow in working with other people? What truths are worthy of preservation and defense, and fostering in others? Your values might be such things as "integrity and truthfulness in all my dealings," "customer interests always come first," "commitment to gender equality," "decisions based on facts, not personal preference," or "creating value by embracing prudent risks." You will also have values about your nonworking life—about the importance you attach to family, community, patriotism, broader social causes, and so on.

As we saw in earlier chapters, leading vision, people development, or cultural change will necessarily reflect your values. So will most of the kinds of strategy development and transformational work you undertake. Values confer credibility and build trust—people know what you stand for. Anne Mulcahy's turnaround of Xerox was successful because she was a longtime employee who deeply believed in the values of the company, so her people knew the changes she demanded were in service of protecting Xerox itself. Similarly, Roger Ferguson's personal commitment to the welfare of people serving those who serve others gave him the credibility to evolve TIAA so its business model could adapt to external financial pressure yet provide its customers with the financial security that the company has provided them for 100 years.

Aspirations and personal resilience

How high do you want to reach for success? How brave will you be, and how hard will you work to get there? When you fall short or suffer a setback in your job, do you have the heart and stomach to work through defeat and the humility to learn, change course, and try again? Do you believe the prizes—tangible and intangible—are worthy and worth what you're willing to endure? Do you have the courage to answer yourself honestly?

Bumble Bee Seafoods CEO Chris Lischewski summarized succinctly what we've heard many times from executives: "Probably the single most important thing for a leader is to have the drive to win and the grit to keep going." Mulcahy recalls that she had to take criticism from all sides at every step of the way, even as she worked as hard as she ever did in her life. Her success in the venture was as much about her personal resilience as any specific strategy. McChrystal reflected how the devastating loss of troops to Al Qaeda terrorism drove him to make personally painful decisions about his leadership identity and to take the gut-wrenching risk of letting go of centralized control so his frontline operatives could strike back faster.

Memories of defeats and bad decisions always loom large in a leader's mind. But the most successful leaders learn profoundly from those, build personal capacity to recover, and then reach higher the next time. As one experienced executive we know reflected, "If you want to be a CEO, you have to endure at least a few really bad days every month. And then learn from them. If you can't handle that, take your ambitions down a few notches." As you strive for higher levels of leadership, keep reflecting on the character you are building through the toughest tumbles of your everyday work. Understand your willingness and ability to rise to the challenges you are setting for yourself.

Your personal style and habits

Are you a take-charge kind of leader? Or are you more reserved and collaborative in getting things done? Are you a people person who readily picks up on others' feelings and emotions, or are you more analytical, using concepts to build relationships? How about your mode of working? Are you supremely organized in all that you do or more situation-dependent in planning and structure?

The answers to these and similar questions will define your style and habits as a leader. If your character represents your inner drive and values, style and habits are the outward signals you send to others. They shape how other people see and work with you; thus, they too are things you must understand about yourself. We see a lot of leadership books, blogs, and seminars focusing on the right ways for a leader to act. But we believe that there's too much human variation in the world to define any simple menu for excellence. Different, very successful leaders often have very different external styles and habits (compare, for example, Winston Churchill and Mahatma Gandhi).

Instead of prescribing a must-have list, we would encourage you to discover your own list by reflecting on what's made you successful thus far. If you're reading this book, you already have some level of accomplishment (and we also know you are looking for more). As you look ahead, consider what attributes of your current style and habits will keep helping you succeed and which might be holding back your future growth.

Holding the external mirror up to yourself

Organize your reflection by again probing with some well-targeted questions, for example, asking yourself and people you work with about the style and habits you bring to your leadership. Many leaders work with a coach or external consultants, using established assessment tools (e.g., Meyers-Briggs, DISC, 360-degree feedback, etc.) to help uncover their workplace behaviors and style. These can be helpful, but you can also structure a basic inquiry for yourself—for example, by adapting Peter Drucker's self-diagnostic from his landmark HBR article "Managing Oneself."

Drucker suggested that all leaders should seek to understand—and then manage and improve upon—self-knowledge in several domains. One of these domains, captured in the question "What are my values?" is part of character, which we've already discussed. But some of his other questions can help you understand critical dimensions of your leadership style and habits.

As you pursue such a diagnostic, what you hear from other people may be different from what you currently believe about yourself. But you have as much to learn from those differences as from the findings themselves.

WHEN AM I MOST EFFECTIVE? Start your self-analysis by simply asking others, "When do you think I'm at my best as a leader?" The intent of this question is to identify specific situations in which you excelled in your recent work.

Listen for patterns in the specific examples your colleagues provide when they think you have been "hitting on all cylinders" as a leader, and then step back and reflect on why they said that and what seems to have made your actions so powerful to them. Also consider if these situations seemed as productive and lively to you as to them. If not, are you missing something about a particular style you brought to the task or some repeatable approach that others apparently found so helpful? For example, did you model the kind of work you expected of others in a tough situation?

Did you stop and draw a picture or chart for everyone that suddenly made your argument clear? Did you stage a debate of opposing views before making a good decision?

Once you've identified patterns of actions that made you excel, ask yourself how you can perform those actions more regularly and deliberately.

WHEN AM I LEAST EFFECTIVE? Inquire also about the opposite case: in leading others, when did I behave in a way that was counterproductive? What stylistic manner or habits do I practice that may put people off, slow progress in a team, or lessen trust for our organization?

You may have to press people to be candid, as you ask them to take on the uncomfortable task of giving you negative feedback. Here again, a third-party-administered survey or set of interviews is sometimes needed to surface the hard truths. But there is often more learning for leaders on this side of the coin, so don't shy away from the opportunity. The feedback you get should prompt your own reflection about your patterns of action and how you can modify them to become more effective.

HOW WELL DO I HANDLE RELATIONSHIPS? Asking about your style and habits of dealing with people is worth its own separate question, even if the topic has already come up in your self-inquiry. Interpersonal relationships are such a large part of leadership that there's value in gaining whatever additional detail you can discover.

In recent years, research on leadership has increasingly highlighted the importance of emotional intelligence in leadership, which we talked about in chapter 3 in reference to building a team. Emotional intelligence, however, also applies to you; it is a major aspect of effective relationship management as first detailed in Daniel Goleman's HBR article "What Makes a Leader?" As you probe others to understand how well you handle relationships, ask about Goleman's component themes: Am I self-aware in a way to understand how my behavior affects others? Do I self-regulate impulses and emotions that are disruptive? How well do I inspire others? Do I bring empathy to bear to understand other people's emotional makeup?

Do I have skills and style to build rapport with others and positively influence action? Where am I strongest, and less strong? Why?

HOW SHOULD I BEST POSITION MYSELF TO DO THE WORK? Given what you have learned about when you are most and least effective and how you handle relationships, how should you shape the role that you play, and the context you operate in, so you can be your best? Leaders will usually have some choice in their roles and work arenas—or better yet, will create some choice for themselves—so they can be as productive and effective as possible.

What kinds of contributions play to your strengths? Can you delegate responsibility in others to complement your efforts, especially where you have less skill or energy? Can you create the kind of working environment—both around you and more broadly in the organization—in which others can thrive to support or add to what you do? Can you take on different roles from time to time so that you can learn and renew yourself or see the business from different perspectives over time?

Authenticity—or not?

Examining your style and habits will likely lead you to the concept of authenticity. In today's workplaces, many people praise leaders who seem authentic, meaning that they seem comfortable in their own skin or don't act at odds with who they really are. Sometimes, people simply mean someone who has a relaxed style or is informal in a personable way. Sometimes, authenticity can also be invoked as an excuse for an objectionable manner, as in "he's rude and very emotional, but hey, at least he's authentic," or to justify various kinds of unfiltered behavior by a leader, even one who can be abusive or uncaring for others.

The original definition of the concept was more nuanced and organizationally constructive. In their classic HBR article "Discovering Your Authentic Leadership," Bill George, Peter Sims, Andrew N. McLean, and Diana Mayer insisted—as we do, too—that it's not helpful to stipulate some cookie-cutter ideal of leadership behaviors that might not fit who you are as an individual. Instead, the authors argue that the best leaders—

authentic leaders—demonstrate a consistent passion for their purpose, build long-standing personal relationships, and know who they are and what makes them unique. We similarly believe that no leader benefits by presenting an artificial and unnatural persona to their organization. Doing so hampers trust and saps motivation of others to collaborate and follow.

At the same time, leadership always requires sensitivity to context; over time, the best leaders also evolve and grow into larger responsibilities, as they take on bigger and more complex challenges. As Herminia Ibarra wrote in an HBR article "The Authenticity Paradox," if as a leader, you are too rigid in allegiance to authenticity, it can stifle the personal growth you'll need to achieve even more significant impact in your career. Leaders must find a middle ground, staying true to who they are, but also be willing to go "beyond one's comfort zone to keep learning and adapting to . . . complex and new situations."

Indeed, many leaders we've talked to endorse authenticity but also stress that they have adapted their own style and habits as conditions required. Stanley McChrystal, in building the empowered network of Special Operations units to fight terrorists in Iraq, "had to unlearn the habit of demanding approvals before all lethal actions, because our strategy depended on giving more authority to our front line." Jeanne Crain, CEO of Bremer Financial Corporation, headquartered in St. Paul, Minnesota, recalls how artificial she felt when, earlier in her career, she was trying to fit into a male-dominated banking culture by wearing mannish suits and accessories such as a pink knit tie, but "also realized being authentic is not about sharing everything you feel inside or showing all aspects of your individuality. It does mean acting in ways that are true to who you are. I had to learn to find those aspects of my own style that would best shape the culture of performance I was trying to build at the bank."

Your knowledge and skills

What are the concrete things you need to know to do your job today? And to do the job you'd like to have after that? What skills will help you take that knowledge and convert it into action? How will they change in the future? Where do you excel and where do you have gaps?

Somewhat more tangible than character, but less visible than style and habits, is knowledge: the understanding—of facts, technical information, industry context, and drivers of performance—that you gain through life and work experience or more formal study. Knowledge is usually passively held in your mind, whereas skills are more hands-on, reflecting how you apply knowledge in practice. For example, as a medical student, you can have the knowledge to do heart surgery—understand how the organ is structured, the patterns that indicate health or disease, and so on—but the skills to work as a cardiologist lie in how you wield the scalpel, make the right kind of incisions, or take emergency action if things go wrong.

In business, you can acquire a lot of knowledge through study, observation, or storytelling by others, but you might still lack the analogous skills to put such knowledge into action. For example, in strategy making, you might have learned lots of different frameworks in business school, but you can't really claim to be skilled at the practice unless you've led a strategy-development process and had to make and live with the kind of tough choices it demands. As you self-assess your knowledge and skills as a leader, remember the differences between those and be honest in evaluating how good or not so good you are at each.

The practices we've introduced in the previous chapters require certain knowledge and skills to perform well. In table 6-1, we summarize some of the most important. The list is a good starting point, but you can add to it as you reflect on your own organizational and developmental context. You can use this rubric as a basis for your self-assessment as you consider your relative strengths and gaps.

Many of the skills and knowledge listed will apply to more than one of the core practices; others will weave through all of them, like emotional intelligence, communications and influence skills, general knowledge of business and the industry you work in, relevant trends shaping competition for your company, and so on. Develop a list of knowledge and skills you think are most important for success in your job and then use that to start assessing what you have, what you lack, and what you need to strengthen or build upon.

TABLE 6-1

Sample knowledge and skills for your leadership practices

Practice	Knowledge	Skill
Building a unifying vision	Your company's aspirations, competitive position, and sources of strength from which to create a future picture of success	Creative thinking, storytelling, effective use of analogies and visual thinking, ability to synthesize ideas and manage conflicts or disagreements in developing a consensus
Developing a strategy	Customer needs, structures of markets, industry trends, competitive landscape	Intelligence gathering, analysis, problem solving, creative thinking, decision making
Getting great people on board	Talent markets, recruiting and development practices, top team management, compensation models	Salesmanship, coaching, giving feedback, negotiating incentives
Focusing on results	Performance management systems and approaches, relevant metrics needed by strategy, best practices fostering collaboration, how to link strategy to operations	Negotiation skills to invest people with accountability, giving tough feedback, resolving conflicts, motivating individuals and groups, decision making
Innovating for the future	Current business models and customer segments, competitive threats and innovation trends, emerging new-business models, markets, technologies	Managing change, managing conflict, both/and thinking, analyzing trade-offs, learning from failure, experimentation
Leading yourself	General knowledge of business, your industry, and company's history; broader trends in the operating environment	Emotional intelligence, communicating for influence and motivation, building trust, time management and prioritization

Getting the outside perspective

Even more than for your character and personal style, soliciting regular outside feedback is a critical step in gaining self-awareness about where you need to build your skills and knowledge. Whereas informal suggestions about adjusting your style are often brief and nonthreatening ("It would be helpful to be more patient when listening to objections from subordinates"), comments about your knowledge and skills might seem to cut directly to your competence as a leader ("You really need to improve your understanding of finance"). Colleagues may be much less likely to speak up about these organically. Furthermore, one of the greatest dangers you face as a leader is not knowing what you don't know, and a gap described in writing can be more specific and powerful than relying on informal spoken feedback.

To organize more formal and written feedback for yourself, arrange for an anonymous and consultant-guided 360-degree feedback survey or a more open-ended set of interviews. Or take steps to ensure that any formal business review of performance also includes constructive assessment of your personal contributions and shortfalls so you can learn and do better in the future.

In any case, whether via informal or more formal feedback, leader after leader whom we interviewed stressed the critical value of hearing constructive suggestions from others to improve their effectiveness. For example, Ferguson of TIAA built a strong working relationship with his top team, which ultimately had the confidence to advise him to shift more of his time and attention to strategic direction versus digging into operational details. John Martin of Innography listened to some trusted subordinates who convinced him that his strong analytical skills as a leader disappeared when he lost his temper. Bob Proctor, both a venture investor and technology CEO, listened to both subordinates and customers say in various private conversations that he needed to get more specialized help in building processes to complement the strategic thinking he was providing as a leader. Paula Kerger of PBS looked forward to hearing "the often strong medicine" of her annual leadership review by the company's board of directors, because, as she commented, "that kind of feedback was the only way I could really understand what I had to do to get better as a leader." She remembers, for example, how the "board gave me a candid assessment of my options when it was time to replace my COO, who had been ill for almost six months. It was a hard personal decision for me, but I had to learn more about managing institutional risk, for example, the institutional vacuum if I were suddenly hit by a bus. While the board encouraged me to act, they also made it clear that the decision was mine."

Questions to Consider: Knowing Yourself

We conclude this section with summary questions that you can use—either for your-self or to guide a third-party assessment of your work—to help you better under-stand who you are as a leader and thus surface critical implications for your future development.

- Consider some specific leaders you admire. What purpose, values, and aspirations do they seem to have? Which do you have too? What are the dif-ferences between theirs and yours? Why?

- Reflect on a few of your career setbacks. What did you learn from the expe-rience? Did you grow and improve from it? Why or why not?

- If you asked key stakeholders about your leadership style, what would they say you should do more of to be more effective? What should you do less of? What should you keep doing the same?

- Describe your authentic self? Are there aspects at odds with where you want to go in the future? Why?

- What knowledge and skills are most critical to your job today? Why? How would key stakeholders—colleagues, partners, customers, employees, and board members—assess your abilities in those? What would they say are your real strengths and biggest gaps?

- When you ask for feedback about yourself, how ready are you to hear something negative? How could you improve any defensive reactions?

Growing yourself

You have now examined who you are and what you're good at and not so good at as a leader; the next step is to think about how to keep improving.

New skills and complex bodies of knowledge can be difficult to mas-ter, but the first challenge for you is to take the time to intentionally work on self-improvement. Many leaders brush aside learning opportunities because they feel as if they distract from their real work. Successful leaders can also fall prey to overconfidence; their achievements of the past trick them into believing more will keep coming, on autopilot. It's a dangerous and false hope.

As you rise in your career, winging it simply won't be enough to meet the level of performance that more senior roles require. The greater the impact you want to have, the more complex the challenges you'll face and the wider the range of knowledge and skills you'll have to develop. You may also need to think more deeply about your willingness to evolve some of your values or to adapt your authentic self, if that's what it takes to succeed in a different kind of organization, or in a bigger and more difficult leadership role.

Because they eagerly confront these challenges, the best leaders are intellectually curious, continually expanding their horizons so that they can think differently about problems. They can reshape their goals, values, and aspirations, as needed. They can open up new opportunities for themselves and their businesses. Being purposeful about further development—and at least a little humble that, yes, you do have new things to learn—is a necessary step to achieving higher personal performance. And though continual learning is very demanding, it also provides renewal and personal satisfaction.

Furthermore, part of your role as a leader is to keep raising the bar of performance for others across your organization. To keep pushing for higher performance all around, you have to set an example of performing and learning yourself—and to keep getting smarter about what "better" means for the whole business—even if you don't become an expert in each domain.

Choosing an approach for learning

There are many different tools, programs, and educational products for learning and professional development, variously suited to different objectives for building your leadership capabilities. What's most important, before you begin, is to be clear about what you're trying to achieve in any course of self-improvement. That will help you choose the most appropriate and cost-effective approach.

In broad terms, we can divide the world of professional development into two major categories: formal learning and informal or on-the-job learning. We'll discuss these in turn and highlight the kinds of knowledge and skills each can best help you develop.

Formal learning

Formal learning has historically meant classroom-style instruction and lecture, supplemented with reading and discussion. Recent evolutions in education have expanded and blurred the category, which now also encompasses computer-assisted content delivery and engagement, online video instruction, role-playing and simulations, and so forth. But the heart of the approach remains the same: someone experienced in a discipline presenting well-codified knowledge to students looking to learn and assimilate what's being offered.

Training and classroom teaching in business are often derided for being too academic and burdensome, but both still have their place, particularly when now enhanced with participatory and individualized experience of technological enhancements. Formal learning can be especially cost-effective for any topic where the facts and practices are well established, or where the knowledge you need to master is sufficiently detailed or technical to make learning on your own, or through episodic experience, less effective (or even impossible). These topics include essential business basics or technical knowledge like accounting, corporate finance, marketing, or different legal topics such as intellectual property or labor law. Formal learning can also be a good way to get up to speed on established best practices in such topics as talent management processes, workplace diversity, compensation policy, and so forth.

Workshop-style programs, which are more participative and facilitated, can help you hone behavioral and stylistic skills such as communicating for influence, giving performance feedback, resolving conflicts, or developing interpersonal strategies for negotiation. The safe space of a workshop or classroom, combined with a program of simulation or case-study learning, can be an excellent way to develop and practice such skills, without the risk of what could become punishing failure in an actual workplace setting.

Participating in university programs or other research-oriented institutions (think tanks, business consortium institutes, etc.) can help build your knowledge and awareness of future trends in industry, society, global economics, and similar areas, critical inputs to inform your company's strategy. Most forward-looking leaders also find time to participate in selected industry or media-sponsored conferences that bring together thought leaders, pace-setting executives, and key policy makers to hear their visions of major emerging issues, emerging innovation, and the shape of leading practice. These, too, can help you shape strategies, performance benchmarks, and plans for your own business.

Informal or on-the-job learning

Despite the potential benefits of formal learning, most of your development as a leader will come—as it should—more informally, from experience you gain on the job. We generally share the bias of learning by doing voiced by the many successful executives we've spoken with for this book. Gary Rodkin, former CEO of ConAgra Foods, attributed his professional rise not to "the thousands of books" on leadership that he was exposed to, but rather specific experiences in which he had to stretch himself, starting early in his career.

While classroom and book learning are particularly effective for acquiring codified information, facts, and well-established practice, we believe that leadership requires something different: more nuanced and contingent skills, judgment, and situation-specific agility that leaders must bring to complex and often unique challenges. This kind of know-how is best honed through personal experience, observation, and reflection.

Learning by doing will be best, for example, in helping you discover—as you articulate and explain to others or must demonstrate through action—your own values and purpose. People will see and you will affirm different aspects of your character for them and yourself. You'll test, refine, and confirm, through practice and reflection, the behaviors and habits that seem to be the most effective for you and that you want to model to others around you.

Similarly, only through trial and application will you appreciate the differences between book-explained versions of a particular strategy or innovation approach, and what it takes to implement them and make them real and understood across a large organization. And only through actual practice can you make abstract theories and ideas of cutting-edge business part of how you think—for example, what a platform strategy really looks like, how to develop a product co-created with customers, how a workforce diversified in its thinking can really perform better. Similarly, only through actual practice can you build the judgment of decision making or develop the emotional intelligence of hearing and accommodating tough feedback about what you do. Only through practice can you develop resilience and grit when you are forced to overcome failure. The daily work you do is a living laboratory that teaches you who you are and who you are trying to become.

What and where to learn on the job

Because on-the-job learning is such a powerful opportunity to grow your leadership capability, you need to leverage that experience intentionally. By simply doing whatever job you have, you are acquiring new insights about yourself and what you need to perform better, but the learning is most effective if you can be conscious about that and not simply accept it as a background benefit of drawing a paycheck.

To be more intentional and productive about on-the-job learning, consider first the "what" and "where" of the experience you are building up: what you need to learn and where you plan to learn it. In terms of the "where," consider two types of arenas: when you are stretching yourself in your current job and then also when you take on different or new responsibilities, whether in your current organization or somewhere new. Such opportunities, properly embraced, can stretch you even further and build deeper and broader skills as you face unfamiliar and more difficult challenges.

LEARNING IN YOUR CURRENT JOB. Every role has the potential to teach you new things. If you're a midlevel manager or rising executive, take full advantage of what you can learn from your boss or supervisor (even the negative lessons or tough feedback about how you performed). Do the same with peers, customers, and people who report to you. If you are a CEO or are already a senior leader, look to your company's board or other external partners who work with you for constructive feedback about what you do. Use performance reviews to keep assessing where you need to improve, and always discuss how you might work on what the findings report. In general, you should make a habit of seeking opportunities to collect feedback from a wide range of people you work for and work with about your performance, style, strengths, and gaps, and generally how you can be more effective as a leader. Listening and keeping yourself open to feedback are your most precious learning tools.

Look also for opportunities to gain specialized learning from, for example, high-profile company initiatives that you have a chance to join in your current functional capacity. Work with your manager to be placed on, say, a new strategic problem-solving task force or a board-sponsored initiative to open up a new market or product development process. If there's some particular knowledge or skill you want to get better in, reach for the appropriate team assignment. Similarly, if you become involved in setting a vision and developing strategy for your company, see that as an opportunity to get smarter about industry trends, changes in the operating environment, market and customer shifts, and so forth. Your time is precious, but don't outsource all that learning to the consultants. Doing some of the research and trend analysis yourself will only add to your own professional knowledge and insights.

Take advantage also of any broader organizational learning initiatives in your company, for example, after-action reviews staged at the end of a major initiative, product launch, or merger. If you've been a decision maker in some corporate initiative under review, have the courage to hear and learn from what you yourself might have done better.

Sometimes learning experiences find you, whether or not you're ready for them. Facing and handling a crisis that comes your way can become what Warren Bennis and Robert Thomas describe in their 2002 HBR article "Crucibles of Leadership" as a "crucible experience"—a major shock, an external catastrophe, or a plunge into bankruptcy, or similar—where a leader must rapidly acquire the knowledge and skills to conquer adversity.

Great leaders embrace such challenges as a source of personal development and a way to make themselves stronger for future opportunities.

If you're serious about learning by doing, you also have to be prepared to fail, just like the skier who falls on the slope and then readies herself to do better in the turns and moguls that lie ahead. If you only put yourself in situations where you succeed, you won't learn resilience and adaptability. You won't learn how to get up, brush yourself off, reflect on what went

Learning from failure

For any organization to perform better, it has to know how to learn from failure, as we have seen in our innovation practice. Learning how to fail and rebound personally is similarly critical for your own career success as a leader. As Ron and his coauthors explained in the HBR article "Rebounding from Career Setbacks," a critical factor in surviving career setbacks—such as not getting a desired promotion, or even getting laid off—is the ability to step back, reflect on what happened, learn from the experience, and then move on. People who spend their time blaming others or feeling victimized are more likely to have another setback or to fall short of their career expectations.

This doesn't mean that you should lower your performance standards and accept that failure is always OK. Unless you're doing an intentional experiment where you actually want to fail a number of times (because it tells you what doesn't work), leadership failure is not something to plan for your agenda. It is, however, inevitable, particularly in complex organizational settings that involve unpredictable human beings and a volatile, rapidly changing environment. Even the best leaders don't get everything right. So when something does go wrong, they use it as a springboard for learning. They reframe the experience around self-improvement, so they don't make the same mistake again and they also have more insight into similar or related situations in the future.

wrong, and then try a different approach. (See the box "Learning from failure.")

LEARNING FROM EVERY NEW JOB. Leaders we've worked with emphasize how much they learned throughout their careers by taking different assignments and facing various kinds of problems and challenges. Whether in new positions in different functions within their existing companies or other responsibilities in other organizations (usually bigger jobs), effective leaders use job rotations and external moves as learning opportunities and then stepping-stones to even greater growth in the future. Xerox's Mulcahy leveraged the skills, people relationships, and cultural credibility she earned by doing years of sales and also a stint in human resources. Ferguson brought sophistication about asset management and market risk to his job leading TIAA from his years at the US Federal Reserve. In her 2010 book *The Corporate Lattice*, Deloitte researcher Cathy Benko summarized this trend of development through different kinds of roles and positions. Her research demonstrated how the traditional practice of moving up a well-established corporate ladder is now giving way to leaders pursuing a zigzag career along something more like a "corporate lattice" across the organization. So seek out opportunities to take on very different kinds of functional roles when you can to broaden your skill set and exposure to different classes of problems.

Keep pursuing this kind of learning, even in the later stages of your career. For example, when biopharmaceutical companies Merck and Schering-Plough merged in 2009, Adam Schechter, who was the head of Merck's global pharmaceutical marketing and the US pharmaceutical business at the time, agreed to take on the role of integration leader. He volunteered, not knowing what this new job would entail, but he saw the new assignment as a personal stretch and a chance to develop his skills for a broader leadership role. As he told us, "I remember going home that night and taking out a blank sheet of paper and saying, 'What do I do tomorrow?'" (see Ron's HBR article, with coauthors Suzanne Francis and Rick Heinick, "The Merger Dividend").

No matter where you are in your career, you can put yourself in stretch situations that foster leadership learning. For example, whatever your role, you can volunteer to assemble a team to tackle a recurring problem, offer to take the lead in resolving a customer or supplier issue, or plan and orchestrate the agenda for a visiting executive. If you can't readily find a business issue, then lead a fund-raising campaign in your office or organize a social event. You also can look outside your current organization for leadership roles in community, religious, or civic groups. All these situations are microcosms of leadership responsibility, requiring you to rally a group of people around a common objective. So they are great laboratories where you can learn how to lead or lead better and differently than you do today.

But in choosing your opportunities, take care that the learning will be robust, that the situations you'll take on will be making you at least a little bit uncomfortable—where you're not quite sure what to do, and where you have to figure it out as you go along. Exposing yourself to well-chosen but new functional and industry challenges will always bring some constructive stretching, but so will taking on a lot more responsibility in areas you're already familiar with. Look for both kinds of settings along the way.

How to learn on the job

Maximizing the benefit of different assignments is, however, not just about the diversity, depth, and breadth of exposures. It also comes from the way you assimilate the experience. So consider not just what you'll learn and where, but also how you'll do it.

In simple terms, this should center on the timeless cycle of human learning that is core to our concept of leadership as a continuing practice: taking action, followed by observation and reflection about results and why you delivered (or failed to deliver) a particular outcome, and then planning and integrating the necessary personal change into your habits to improve the next time.

Our most fundamental advice is to be intentional: whatever your job, be mindful about the decisions and actions you are taking to perform your work. Take time periodically to observe, analyze, and think about how a particular initiative worked out. Synthesize and put into words what succeeded or fell short, and why. Resolve, based on what you see and understand, what you should do differently or better the next time. Hold yourself accountable to that.

The most obvious actor in all this is you. Your observation and reflection can be greatly helped by listening for feedback from others or engaging in after-action reflection with people you trust, for example, an informal mentor or an executive coach. Many professionals also find it is valuable to keep a journal or, for less personally sensitive experience, to write a blog or share thoughts with a more public audience through other forms of social media. Many executives also develop informal learning relationships with a volunteer group of peer practitioners (typically from noncompetitive organizations in the same industry) and engage in regular exchange about each member's professional experience, learning from one another in the format of a so-called community of practice (see Etienne Wenger and William Snyder's HBR article "Communities of Practice: The Organizational Frontier").

LEARN FROM OTHERS. In addition to self-observation and reflection, there's also plenty to learn secondhand—by watching and analyzing the practices and style of other leaders. Begin with your own boss or other senior people in your organization: look beyond the direction they are setting or the work they might be creating for you, and think about their skills or mistakes as leaders per se. If one delivers an important speech to the organization, how did it go? Why? When you're hearing feedback from your boss, apart from the content of what they told you, how did they handle the overall situation? Did they leave you feeling more or less energized? When you have to do the same thing with more junior people, what would you do differently—and why? Looking through a self-improvement lens, you can start to see your whole organization and the earlier stages of your career as one big learning laboratory. As John Lundgren at Stanley Black & Decker thoughtfully remarked, "A lot of what I learned about leadership came from watching and learning from a couple of terrific bosses in my earlier career and also vowing never to act like one very bad one whom I also once had."

THE VALUE OF AN EXECUTIVE COACH. We've mentioned the potential value of working with an executive coach. If you've never had the opportunity to do so, here are some suggestions to help you get started.

First, as John Baldoni explains nicely in his HBR article "Before Working with a Coach, Challenge Your Self-Assumptions," deliberately articulate for yourself why you're looking for some outside help and what specifically you hope to get out of the relationship. Recognize and manage the engagement as a growth opportunity, as Ron describes in his HBR article "If Your Boss Tells You to Get a Coach, Don't Panic." Understand also that not all executive coaches are the same. Beyond the chemistry of a relationship you might want to find, realize that different coaches bring different approaches and have different kinds of expertise. For example, some may focus on interpersonal skills, others on strategic thinking, still others on personal productivity, and so on. Be clear with yourself—and your potential coach—on what you expect and need.

Second, a more subtle point, understand that an executive coach is only one part of a larger system of personal growth (see Marshall Goldsmith and Gardiner Morse's HBR article "Behave Yourself"). A good coach will help you reflect and recognize things you may not see or realize about yourself, and may also help you synthesize and plan how to improve against specific professional or personal challenges. But remember, the coach is not the only one who is going to offer feedback to you and will sometimes be more of an aggregator than originator of relevant insights. Often the most important feedback for you will come not from the voice of the coach but from the words of colleagues, supervisors, partners, and customers. Similarly, don't expect the coach to do the work of changing you for the better. Improvement only comes through your own actions and commitment; the coach may guide and challenge you, but real leadership transformation starts and ends with you.

A summary of general learning principles

As you weigh—and then participate in—different opportunities for growth and self-improvement as a leader, follow some general principles:

- **Balance building on strengths and shoring up weaknesses.** Much research shows that the payback for professional development is higher when you focus less on remediating weaknesses and more on leveraging your strengths, especially those that drive the most value for your organization. But as Robert Kaplan and Robert Kaiser have also shown in their HBR article "Stop Overdoing Your Strengths," your strengths can be overdone, and you can become a lopsided and ineffective leader if you keep developing and pushing them to excess. It's much better to work on creating a balance between what you do well and not so well, and continue to solicit feedback about "what should I do more of, what less of, to be effective?"

- **Go beyond your comfort zone.** As we've said, learning and growth come from being stretched and confronted with new and difficult challenges. Be willing to engage in professional development where you may not be the boss, where you hear things that might criticize your style and performance, or where you are in unfamiliar situations.

  There are limits, however: beware joining programs to build a skill clearly far beyond your current capability. You need to be stretched, not broken or humiliated, to learn. Also beware of would-be development programs that promise some kind of mystical self-understanding or that pose significant physical risk with a false promise, for example, "walking on burning coals at our company retreat will truly teach you about self-control" (this was once a real trend in team-building circles).

- **Be intellectually humble and listen, listen, listen.** Unless you are open to new ideas and challenges, you will never grow. Too many leaders suffer from overconfidence that closes their minds to acquiring new skills and knowledge. So develop the habit of erring on the side of listening to others and not always speaking first.

Throughout your career, you will constantly be engaging with employees, customers, board members, partners, and other stakeholders. See each as a source of potential learning about trends, innovations, and problems to fix and about ways of working as a leader where you've excelled or fallen short. You will hear challenges to how you work, critiques of how you think, and a steady stream of suggestions for why and how you can do better. See those discussions as a resource, not an attack on your prestige.

- **Practice the traditional learning cycle.** We stress again that time-tested research has shown that people learn and develop by following an iterative cycle of acting, then assessing the results, reflecting on why those happened, and then taking steps to improve from the learning. Whenever you are trying to develop new skills or knowledge, structure a process that honors the cycle.

- **Match the learning opportunity to the need and to your learning style.** Different programs and experiences are suited to different professional challenges, as we've described. But as you engage in any opportunity, be mindful of your own learning preferences. People with more introverted personalities often prefer to read or study on their own; extroverts enjoy group conversation and engagement. Visual tools and experiences are very important to some people, less to others. You may insist on analytical presentation or prefer more experiential or intuitive learning. Know what works and doesn't work for you, and make that part of your development planning.

- **Prefer learning and development that pertain to real work and your current challenges.** As a general rule, learning that is more directly relevant to the actual work you are doing and satisfies immediate skill or knowledge needs will be more meaningful and impactful for you. And it's the kind of learning that most leaders make time for.

Questions to Consider: Growing Yourself

Growing yourself professionally is the single best investment you can make to become a leader, but the job is ultimately in your hands, not anyone else's. If you're wise, you'll be learning constantly from other people every day, but steering the journey in a way that builds the important skills and knowledge that you most need. Here's a short self-diagnostic to help you get started and to take control of your own development. You can use it throughout your career:

- After self-assessing your character, style, and knowledge, where are the greatest opportunities for growing yourself? What are your strengths to build upon, and what's holding you back? How will you find the right balance in managing strengths and weaknesses?

- What formal and informal opportunities for learning and improving in the coming year would provide you with the opportunities you identified?

- How can you get feedback from your different stakeholders more consistently, as a regular part of your job? Should you consider having a formal coach or take some other action to get ongoing professional advice?

- Are there specific industry or functional conferences to attend or other sources of new strategic and market knowledge you should pursue? Which offer the right value for time and money invested?

- Can you develop peer relationships in your industry or create a community of practice for collective learning and support with other professionals doing your kind of work?

- Have you dedicated time to reflect on, write about, or discuss with others your own challenges and accomplishments in personal growth? Are you doing that regularly?

- Can you construct an explicit overall plan to improve yourself in light of all the previous questions? What would your plan for the coming year look like? What priorities and timing will you assign to your goals?

■   What discipline can you bring to ensure your plan doesn't get lost in the everyday hustle of your daily job?

Sharing yourself

Leading yourself is actually not all about *you*. Your growth will also benefit from contributing to the growth and welfare of others—potential leaders or other people in your organization, stakeholders, and beyond—and also volunteering for civic or community organizations, or other causes in which you are personally interested. To lead well, you sometimes need to share yourself. At first glance, this might seem like a distraction from your everyday priorities. But smart leaders reap tangible rewards from sharing themselves with others, and it's a critical part of how they create significant impact.

Opportunities for growing others

An important strategy for leaders to increase the scale and performance of their organization is to develop other leaders, whether a top team or other key players (as we discussed in chapter 3). Coaching, advising, and helping other executives, including rising younger staff in your organization, adds to your company's overall skill and knowledge base. More and stronger leaders pulling together magnifies what any organization can achieve—whether a team, individual unit, division, or the whole enterprise. Even if you are the CEO, you can't do it all. The sooner you identify and enable great help, other leaders who can join you in pursuing the goals you are striving for, the better the long-term results. And other great leaders working with you will help make you personally more effective, too.

Some leaders may be reluctant to develop others around them. They may hold back because of their insecurity, a worry that someone they mentor may someday become more valuable than they are. Or they're simply being selfish in the short term, not wanting to lose valuable professionals who may move on to other opportunities once they develop additional skills. Or it may simply be the result of poor prioritization, not wanting to take the time away from doing everyday real work. But the longer-term dividends of growing others, as well as building more extended networks of relationships for the future, more than justifies the effort and apparent risks. Good leaders never fear helping others grow.

The strategic benefit of mentoring and developing other professionals holds equally true for partners or other members of the value chains on which your company depends. Instead of seeing them only as transactional providers, consider whether helping partner leaders improve their companies' performance wouldn't help you also succeed, too. For example, in the 1990s, Toyota famously invested in training its manufacturing partners, so that working together, they could all make major leaps in quality.

Broadening horizons

Many leaders we have worked with are confident people, motivated by a broad sense of obligation to advance the common good and generally help others. But their volunteer service also enhances their leadership: helping them build skills and extend their personal networks. For example, Dominic Barton of McKinsey keeps himself sharp—and also in touch with interesting people, ideas, and innovations beyond his daily work—by serving as a volunteer at buildOn, an initiative to help inner-city students graduate from high school, along with being a trustee for the Brookings Institution and a director of Memorial Sloan Kettering Hospital and other social and research institutions. Ferguson demonstrates his personal commitment to the educational and research sectors core to TIAA's mission by giving some of his own advisory time to the Smithsonian Institution, the American Academy of Arts & Sciences, the Commission on the Future of Undergraduate Education, and the Institute for Advanced Study. Such service also builds his relationships with key decision makers across various domains that TIAA serves.

Even a personal interest, properly chosen, can positively redound to your own growth as a leader. John Lundgren, of Stanley Black & Decker, is an inveterate golfer and a director for the golf equipment company Callaway. As he told us, "I love the sport, but it's also instructive for me to help that company wrestle with some pretty challenging business issues."

Guiding principles for sharing yourself

Successful leaders like Dominic Barton, Roger Ferguson, and John Lundgren are in constant demand to advise or serve as volunteers for other organizations, just as they are in their own organizations to help younger leaders with their own development. As you advance in your career, you will experience increasing demand for help from others, too. You'll be forced to keep deciding when and how to step in and lend a hand to other people and institutions, which you may consider for your own short- or long-term interest, or because of some general sense of responsibility of giving back or contributing to a societally valuable institution. Or, all of the above.

How should you make these kinds of decisions as a leader? Where and how much of your precious time should you give to others, beyond your normal day-to-day work? Once again, there's no one-size-fits-all answer, but here are a few guiding principles to help you decide:

- **Be selective, based on value.** You'll have to constantly weigh when to say yes and when to say no to a sharing opportunity, but structure your decision making around some clear and intentional criteria. Evaluate the personal and professional value that you might derive in making the contribution, whether learning, developing new networks, or undertaking some other developmental experience, both short and long term. If there is no immediate benefit for you and you still want to say yes, understand why you think this is still a worthy investment (there's no harm in helping some greater good, but just recognize that's what you're really trying to do). Be clear, also, about whether this opportunity calls on your particular knowledge, skills, or relationships, and whether offering those can really make a positive difference.

- **Be focused enough to have impact.** Unless you can give serious attention to what's being asked of you, it's not worth surrendering your time. It's better to concentrate on a more limited group of people and institutions where you can meaningfully contribute than spread yourself too thin or simply pad your résumé with a list of token volunteering.

- **Diversify your sharing portfolio.** Consider, as many successful leaders do, coaching not just key employees in pivotal roles, but also a sprinkling of more-junior people or people with very different backgrounds than yours—simply to broaden the experience of what you might learn as you contribute. Similarly, consider diversifying the kind of external organizations for which you volunteer or on whose boards you serve to enrich the range of problems and different networks you might potentially encounter.

- **Don't shy away from the occasional open-ended contribution.** As much as you should assess the value you bring and what you also might derive from a sharing opportunity, sometimes it's worth volunteering without a predetermined ROI. Trust your gut if a person or organization calls you in need and answering the request "just seems like the right thing to do." Realize also that helping others and taking yourself into new situations often leads to unexpected and sometimes unrelated opportunities, far beyond anything you would have guessed when you first began. Be a bit speculative with the investment of your time, but don't overdo it.

Questions to Consider: Sharing Yourself

Here's a short self-diagnostic to help you get started as you think about how to respond to demands for your help—and where to proactively give your time to others.

- In what ways are you sharing your knowledge, skills, relationships, or other leadership assets with others today? Where are you having the most impact? Why? Where are you making the most difference for time invested? For those you're helping? For yourself?

- With that in mind, consider whether and how you might expand further— but also better structure—your contribution to developing other people or helping organizations or institutions that you care about. Articulate the rationale for your additional choices and how you will ensure that your time investment is most effective. Are your choices spread across different domains to provide varied experiences and relationships? Have you found a balance between some diversity of learning and not getting spread too thin?

- Are there people or causes or institutions you naturally want to help in some way, regardless of what you might immediately gain from the effort? Who and what institutions are those? What does that tell you about your values and sense of purpose?

Taking care of yourself

Executives we know speak openly about the challenges of preserving their own sense of well-being through the stress and turmoil of their challenging jobs. Many touch on the difficulty of finding time to think amid the day-to-day issues at work. Others concede that their diets, health, and physical stamina suffer from constant travel and too many late nights of constant deadlines or client demands. Others voice frustration that they can't give back as much to society as they want, due to time pressure. And it's common to hear from leaders how hard they find it to spend the right kind of time with family and on other personally meaningful pursuits.

You bring an enormous effort to the tasks of building your organization and your people. So who's taking care of *you* to make sure you don't burn out, get sick, or get so fragmented that everything personal and professional falls to pieces? If you are exhausted, frustrated, ignoring who you are and what you care about, the people and performance you are trying to lead will suffer. You may have a loving partner at home who supports you emotionally and a crackerjack assistant at work who keeps you on schedule, but they can't do it all for you. To be an effective leader, you have to take care of yourself too.

Personal strategies

What kind of personal strategies do you have—or do you need to develop—to be both self-protective and energized as a leader? As the word "personal" suggests, the kind of strategies you develop and follow must be at least somewhat suited to your own preferences and needs. Here again, there's no simple, universal paradigm. But we can identify a few general working approaches that leaders we know have developed to increase their own wellness. In these and many other cases, the solutions for finding wellness in some regard were devised by leaders themselves—understanding what was important to them, setting goals, and problem-solving ideas about how to achieve them (sometimes with peers, family members, an able assistant—or all of the above), and then putting in place mechanisms and rules that they committed themselves to follow. They were intentional about what they did, but often followed certain behaviors intuitively, which is why knowing yourself—where we began this chapter—is so important. If you can truly understand who you are, what your personal priorities are, what matters to you, and what you want to improve about yourself, self-care becomes just one more goal to achieve, adding further to your growth as a leader.

To help you design your own regime, let's look at a few principles leaders employ to preserve and renew themselves.

Routinize common interactions

To avoid duplication and minimize the inevitable frustrations of daily management, don't reinvent processes or assemble time-consuming details repeatedly for tasks that recur throughout your work. For example, to maintain focus and manage demands on her time, Jane Kirkland of State Street Corporation schedules regularly standardized reviews for every initiative she's overseeing (much as in the operational reviews discussed in chapter 4). Kirkland also insists on handling contentious issues or questions that come up only in the meetings dedicated to those, so they don't intrude later and distract from the critical focus of other working sessions. Stan McChrystal created a well-structured and consistent agenda for the daily online global intelligence briefing for the thousands of members of his terrorist-fighting network. The template allowed all participants to prepare to share the kind of information needed and to what end, and the structure also enabled McChrystal to play an appropriate leadership coaching role without having to adjudicate the process as commanding officer.

Partition your time at work

Many successful leaders intentionally partition their schedules to reduce fragmentation and start-and-stop problem solving. Rune Olav Pedersen, president and CEO of PGS (a petroleum geo-services company in Norway), handles requests from junior colleagues in dedicated office hours and declines any meetings that he doesn't absolutely have to attend. Many leaders we know also regularly block their calendars and don't take calls or meetings before 9 a.m. to give themselves needed time to think, write, or engage in personal productivity, such as planning their day or reflecting on progress toward key operational goals.

Partition your time outside of work

Like many others who want to contribute to society beyond their jobs, McKinsey's Dominic Barton allocates regular time working for selected organizations outside of McKinsey and simply has his assistant build his annual schedule around that specific allocation. Others take a similar approach to preserve family bonds. Anne Mulcahy taught her peers and subordinates at Xerox that unless it was a true emergency, they shouldn't call her on weekends at home when she was with her husband and children. Over time, she successfully enforced those boundaries, though it often meant she had to become comfortable with more delegation as her responsibilities became more complex. Tamara and John Lundgren, spouses who are both CEOs of different organizations, optimize every weekend together by making every effort to schedule all face-to-face business meetings with subordinates and clients during the week, including over dinner and sometimes late into the evening.

Simplify and prioritize your decision making

Brains that face too many choices and excessive inflows of information get tired, just as your arm muscles do if you try to do too many push-ups in an hour. In the HBR article "Boring Is Productive," Robert Pozen summarizes that research and recounts the story of Barack Obama, who always wore either a gray or blue suit so he could "pare down his decision making" to focus his thinking on the truly substantive choices he would face during his day. Listen to other effective executives confronted with this or that issue, and you'll frequently hear them say, "That's not a decision I need to make," because either someone closer to the problem can handle it or the stakes of the outcome don't merit the trouble required to make a good judgment. Try bringing the same discipline of appropriate prioritization to other decisions and demands. Just because you're a leader doesn't mean you need to decide everything yourself.

Seek energy-renewing work and activity

In recent years, researchers have increasingly focused on the importance of personal energy in leadership and also the collective energy of organizations more broadly. Though such things may seem intangible, the vim and vigor—both physical and psychological—that you bring to a task, and that you create among others, can dramatically affect the results you achieve, as Tony Schwartz and Catherine McCarthy describe in the classic HBR article "Manage Your Energy, Not Your Time." Not surprisingly, most effective leaders work to build rituals or activities into their schedules that renew their energy and set a tempo for others to follow.

For many leaders, that might begin, for example, by pursuing a discipline of daily exercise, regardless of one's agenda or travel (that's the case for John Martin, Stan McChrystal, Anne Mulcahy, and many others we've worked with), or something more simple, such as meditating in the first hour before your office officially opens, practicing regimes of mindfulness, or a regularly taking a walk in the sunshine at lunchtime.

Some strategies that build and renew energy for leaders stem from choosing—or designing—your work. If certain tasks or kinds of meetings especially drag you down, consider if you can delegate them or move them out of your schedule (admittedly, the answer is sometime no, but at least ask yourself). Roger Ferguson of TIAA gave up some senior administrative tasks, not only because he knew he wasn't as good at those as he was at more strategic work, but also because it directed too much of his energy away from the areas where he felt he could have the biggest impact. Consider also building a schedule that always allows you to do at least some of the work that you love. Dominic Barton, even during his jam-packed tenure as global managing partner of McKinsey, insisted on serving a few clients "because it both kept me in touch with the heart of our strategy and allowed me to keep doing challenging problem-solving that I really enjoy."

Achieving broader balance

As much as these strategies can serve to improve a leader's personal wellness and effectiveness, most executives also acknowledge that self-care involves much more than just improving job productivity. Ultimately taking care of yourself as a leader must also be about recognizing how your work fits into the rest of your life. How do you prioritize between your differing spheres of things personal, professional, and social? How can you best fit them together and achieve some kind of holistic harmony among them?

As we've said, being clear about your personal priorities is always a good first step. Understanding what really matters to you and how, on the margin, you might choose to allocate different segments of your time is a discipline that any leader should adopt. If you think and act as if everything is equally important—work, family, personal growth or interests, spiritual life, and so on—you are essentially saying you don't have any real priorities.

As Ron wrote in the HBR article "How Trivial Decisions Will Impact Your Happiness," the inevitable pull of work once you start achieving success in your job will constantly force you to keep making one small compromise after another versus your nonwork life—missing a child's school recital, forgoing a church or family event you had vowed to be part of, and so forth. That's OK, but only if that's the way you want to intentionally allocate your time on this earth. But maybe constant and shifting compromises are not OK for you. Can you honestly answer what you believe about such choices? Can you be more intentional about identifying and acting on your most meaningful preferences?

Many leaders fail to be explicit with themselves about what their real priorities are. As a leader, you have the right—and obligation—to choose what kind of balance you have in your life. But you need to be clear about what you want. Whether you're looking in a mirror, talking with an executive coach, or writing down goals for your own life plan, be honest enough to confront the following questions: (1) What's the balance I want to have between personal and professional success? (2) If I really had to choose between one or the other, which one do I see as most important? Why? (3) What specific goals do I have in each of these arenas? (4) How do I think about intentionally trading them off?

Once you're formed your answers—and can authentically say they are both true and will be visible in how you will actually act—you can then start to develop pragmatic strategies to reach those goals. In some cases, your strategies might be some simple rules about the core situations when family comes first versus, say, when work comes first—and the rationale for when (and only when) you will make an exception. In other cases, you might institutionalize your priorities with a structured schedule or a set of commitments that you make and review those regularly with your executive coach or mentor. Whatever your approach, the critical step is understanding your goals and having a concrete plan, however simple, to hold yourself accountable to those goals.

Not surprisingly, many smart people have explored questions about finding the right balance or fuller integration among different goals throughout life and work. If you want to be more ambitious in your planning than simply charting a basic work-life balance, you'd be well served to tap into some of the recent thoughtful research. Two frameworks from HBR articles are good options to consult, described in the next section.

Integration: total leadership

In the HBR article "Be a Better Leader, Have a Richer Life," Stewart D. Friedman identifies a framework of four "domains" of life—work, home, community, and self (meaning mind, body, and spirit); these accord well with the cluster of issues we've heard about repeatedly from leaders we've worked with.

Friedman argues that rather than achieving a binary work-life balance, leaders should strive for "total leadership" by creating dynamic integration across all four domains. He recommends that leaders follow a problem-solving and "experimental process." First, talk with key stakeholders in each domain (e.g., at work, with peers and subordinates; at home, with members of your family; and so on). Use the discussions to learn from them about who you are and what matters to you. Then define personal objectives and assess your level of satisfaction against that. Then, over time, develop new rituals, undertake new opportunities, or create other life changes that help you progress toward objectives you have defined in each of the four domains.

As your experiments become more successful, you'll find more opportunities to unify the activities and goals across the four and start to achieve greater harmony in your personal and professional life. Friedman underscores that success in any one of the domains can foster success in any of the others: by practicing your leadership with diverse talents and constituencies in a community setting, for example, you can prime yourself to achieve similar competence at work.

Andrew Géczy, CEO of Terra Firma whom we met earlier in the book, described a similar approach that he has used to take care of himself over the years:

> Once a year I sit down and look at the five dimensions of my life—personal health, relationships with family, relationships with friends, contributions to the community, and achievements at work. I've been doing this for a long time, and each year I try to make conscious decisions about where I want to put more or less of my time and energy, and what trade-offs might be needed. I then share and discuss the five topics with a couple of trusted friends and mentors. It's never a perfect pentagon, and it changes year to year, depending on what's happening with the family, or the job, or my own health. It's not a perfect framework, but it gives me the discipline of reflecting and adjusting among all my priorities at different times.

Setting course: measuring your life

In his landmark HBR article "How Will You Measure Your Life?" renowned Harvard strategist Clayton Christensen proposes a different but comparable framework. Christensen suggests that as a leader, you should identify a handful of essential metrics that define success for your life over-all. He focuses on three questions: How can I be happy in my career? How can I be sure that my relationship with my family is an enduring source of happiness? And how can I live my life with integrity? By setting and then pursuing deliberately a strategy for each, much as you would for an organization, Christensen argues that you can achieve the highest possible outcome in each sphere.

———

Whatever your aspiration and preferred level of work-life integration, taking care of yourself is no less important than other elements of leadership we've discussed in this chapter. Don't neglect it! We close now with one more set of questions to help you get started on this element of the practice.

Questions to Consider: Taking Care of Yourself

How satisfied are you today in your job, with:

- Your personal productivity? How you allocate your time and prioritize your calendar?

- Managing the flow of demands on your time from employees, customers, and other stakeholders?

- Finding the right balance between doing and thinking?

- Really understanding the relative priority of your work versus nonwork life?

- Having the opportunity to consistently maintain your health and level of energy?

- Having enough time with family or friends outside of work?

- Having enough time for social, community, or other civic organizations you care about?

- Having the opportunity to pursue spiritual renewal or engage with personal religious beliefs?

Review your answers to the questions. Think about each issue, especially where you have low satisfaction:

- What's holding you back from higher satisfaction today?

- What are some changes, mechanisms, or new disciplines you could develop to improve your situation?

- Are there people—colleagues, subordinates, assistants, a personal coach—who could help you devise, and then support, your improvement strategies?

- How will you measure your progress, and how can you regularly review that progress to correct course and improve over time?

The practice of leading yourself will at times be a very solo and even lonely journey for you. But it is fundamental to both your personal success and everyone else your leadership will touch. Many leadership books begin—and go no further than—where this volume ends: focusing on self-understanding, critical habits, and other personal aspects of leading yourself. We hope that you see these aspects of the practice as means to an end rather than ends unto themselves. By developing yourself, you develop your ability to achieve collective organizational effectiveness, once again, to deliver greater impact by working with others toward common goals.

Questions to Consider

- **Know yourself.** What key questions should you be asking in order to better know yourself? Are you most confident in your self-assessment of character, style, or skills? Where would it help to get an external perspective?

- **Grow yourself.** What is your preferred style of learning: reading, classroom, on the job, as a mentee? Are you finding ways to maximize that style of learning? Do you have explicit learning goals for the next year or two or three—and a plan to get there?

- **Working with a coach.** Do you have an executive coach or mentor who can help you develop yourself over time? If so, are you getting the candid and sometimes challenging inputs that you need? If you don't have access to a coach, can your friends or colleagues help you overcome your blind spots?

- **Sharing yourself.** Are you mentoring or coaching others inside or outside your organization? Spending time building other leaders? What are you learning from helping others grow?

- **Contributing beyond.** In what ways are you contributing beyond just your immediate job or the boundaries of your current organization? Can you broaden your horizons and get exposure to new ways of thinking by volunteering or engaging in civic ventures?

- **Taking care of yourself.** How are you balancing your commitments to work with whatever else you want to do in terms of family, friends, and activities? Are you being explicit about the trade-offs, or are they just happening over time?

- **Energy and well-being.** What are you doing to take care of yourself physically and emotionally as you progress in your career? Do you have ways of renewing your energy periodically after intense periods of work?

- **Measuring your life and finding balance.** What are your personal metrics of success—not just for this week, month, quarter, or year—but for your life and your career? How can you keep these metrics in perspective as you continue to advance as a leader? What can you do to find greater balance and even integrate different arenas where you spend your time or would like to spend more time?

Conclusion: Putting It All Together

Let's look back to the three rising leaders we met in the introduction of this book. If you were like Linda, the marketing head, and you wondered if becoming a leader required a mystical personality transformation, you now know that it doesn't; it builds on the work you're already doing as a manager. If you were like Linda's friend Sam, the newly appointed COO of a nonprofit who had been assuming that leadership meant just working harder, you now know that, too, is not true. It's about learning how to call upon others, finding ways to mobilize and leverage the efforts of your team and the broader organization. And if you were like Natalie, anxious about launching her own startup, you now understand that you can break the complex challenge of running a big organization into manageable practices, and that you can prioritize those by where you can have the biggest impact. Leadership is something you can do.

To close, we highlight a few major themes that cut across this book and that might help you as you reflect on (and begin practicing) the practices.

Leadership matters

Obviously, human progress doesn't just happen automatically. Yes, some initiatives may be self-organizing, and serendipity and fortune play a role in any outcome, but without leadership, big and important things just don't get done. Without the push and drive of Seraina Macia, XL's North American P&C business would never have started growing again. It took Stanley McChrystal to transform a military organization into an effective network to fight the terrorism of Al Qaeda in Iraq. Jim Smith had the vision, experience, and sense of purpose to guide Thomson Reuters toward a greater focus on growth and innovation.

We are not saying that no one else might have achieved similar results, nor that success for any of these leaders was guaranteed. Instead, we want you to understand, as our case examples and discussions of practices have shown, that large and complicated challenges require lots of people working together on solutions. Leadership is needed to motivate and align that kind of effort. Such challenges are your opportunity to make the fundamental difference that defines a leader. Don't wait to be anointed by someone else. Seize the moment to make yourself a leader.

Think big and bold and look around the corners

Seizing the leadership opportunity and making the leadership difference in fact requires courage and also an ability to look beyond the everyday and near-term tasks of basic management. Remember Dominic Barton, the global managing partner of McKinsey whom we've met throughout the book? In our conversation, he said that managers take care of the railroad tracks, but leaders shift the tracks, change the boundaries, and redefine directions. In other words, the leader's thought process is bigger and bolder and much more forward thinking. To be a leader, you need to anticipate like a great chess player who looks ten moves ahead and also quickly adjusts to the opponent's play.

This doesn't mean that you should completely ignore the current challenges of your organization and focus only on the future. On the contrary, your customers, clients, employees, investors, and partners are all counting on you to keep your eye on the present and ensure that you're doing what's needed to get results. As you do this, however, you can move into leadership by looking at what's next, and what's next after that.

You can apply this thought process to many aspects of management and, in so doing, demonstrate the leadership difference. For example, as you work on setting yearly (or quarterly or monthly) goals for yourself and your team, go beyond ordinary and incremental improvements. Think about what's needed to accelerate progress toward the organization's vision and how your area can contribute. Then challenge your people to get to a whole new level of performance that will not only stretch their capabilities, but also make others take notice. And as you work with your team to achieve these goals, help them prioritize what's important and what's not, facilitate collaboration with other areas, and teach everyone how to work as a team. As you're doing all that, start thinking about the next wave of improvement and beyond. In other words, grasp the leadership opportunities already in your reach and then keep looking beyond.

But also have the courage to let go

Leadership requires guts to seize opportunity but, in that pursuit, also the guts to trust others and not try doing it all yourself. Busyness creates its own sense of psychological comfort, but also an artificial sense of always being needed—and that will leave you with too little time for real leadership.

Tackling any major challenge will overwhelm you if you insist on facing it alone. Learn to delegate to others, for example, investing team members with key tasks that must be done and sharing the burden with—and then not micromanaging—other leaders and professionals committed to the same big goals.

Learn, also, to reach deep into your organization for good ideas and fresh approaches to problems; be open to solutions that come from the bottom up or even from beyond your organization. More and more leaders are embracing "the wisdom of the crowd."

Yes, you'll be taking on some risk as you venture into letting go; the colleagues you trust to help with the work may not do it as well as you think you could. Yes, some people may see your delegation as a sign of your own weakness or inability. Yes, you may feel some twinge of an identity crisis if sharing power or trusting more junior employees or talented outsiders leaves you feeling like you're not really in charge. But achieving big impact always involves some risk, and as a leader, you must consider the opposite—and usually worse—risk of *not* leveraging the best possible ideas, of demotivating colleagues because they have no chance to make their own contribution, of becoming a bottleneck because you want to control everything yourself.

As a leader, you must know yourself, steel yourself, and trust in the best organizational approach you can arrange. It's why Anne Mulcahy was happy to add a few strong strategic thinkers with skills she lacked when she was leading the Xerox turnaround, why Jim Wolfensohn went beyond his executive team and engaged the broader community of the World Bank when developing a new vision, and why Roger Ferguson gave up some operational jobs that could take his attention away from his focus on the evolution of TIAA.

Inspire and demand

Dreaming big and having the courage to pursue those dreams—despite the risk—is essential for leaders. But you also need to get others to share your dream, vision, and purpose. Leadership is about creating significant impact through others, but those others have to be motivated to perform. You can't just tell your people what to do and walk away. They need to understand what you are trying to accomplish, how their work contributes to the broader goal, and how the broader goal will make a difference for them, for your customers, and perhaps for the world. The people you lead need to be inspired, excited, and challenged or they won't follow, and they won't make good decisions in support of the vision when you're not around. "BHAGs" (big, hairy, audacious goals) and "stretch goals" are not just clever terms; they're essential leadership tools for getting your team and your organization to the next level.

Getting everyone charged up is not enough, however. Once your team realizes that the goal isn't easy and that it will take hard, inventive, and persistent effort, you'll also have to provide ongoing encouragement. Leaders believe in their people, that they can achieve even more than they themselves thought possible. The "Pygmalion Principle" made famous in the 1950s musical *My Fair Lady* is worth remembering here: if you expect your people to succeed, they are more likely to live up to your expectations. Conversely, if you constantly second-guess and doubt them, your people will lose their confidence.

Still, you need to temper encouragement with strong demands. You have to make it clear to your people that they have to get results along the way and that there are no rewards for effort alone. Finding the right balance between inspiring and demanding is a constant tension for leaders, and one that you'll probably have to work on throughout your career. It's always tempting to be the good guy, the cheerleader, and the nice leader whom everyone likes. It's tougher to do what Darren Walker did at the Ford Foundation and look people in the eye and tell them that their performance is unacceptable or that they need to upgrade their skills, and that they will be held accountable if they don't change. But if you don't do both, you'll end up with a happy team that doesn't get anything done, which won't make you, your customers, and your investors happy at all.

Learn from your failures

Courage and risk taking, along with inspiring and demanding, are certainly key virtues for leaders, but so is a certain amount of humility. Big, bold moves and trusting others sometimes don't work out, or worse, turn into disasters.

All leaders have their share of setbacks; the key is adopting a mindset of learning from failures and having the resilience to bounce back, wiser and more experienced for the next challenge. Over time, if you just keep working at it, you become a better leader. Thus, Dom Barton's successful collaborative strategy to transform McKinsey was shaped by the trial-and-error approach he took as he was learning to build the firm's practice in Korea. John Lundgren's growth strategy for Stanley Black & Decker went on to even bigger success after he and his team learned from a major setback they had in a badly failed European acquisition. Stan McChrystal's idea about the new network approach to his Middle East command grew out of several initial defeats suffered at the hands of his more nimble terrorist enemy.

Create an organization of one mind

For all the personal boldness, risk taking, challenging, and learning you must embrace as a leader, you must also build a collective organization of people who are as passionate, committed, and dedicated to performance as you are. Your goal, stated more simply, is to create a one-minded pursuit of excellence. Great leaders work tirelessly to motivate and align large masses of people to achieve the kinds of goals that no individual can accomplish on their own.

Leaders work on this in many ways: by creating a common and motivating vision that all can see and believe in, as Wolfensohn did with the World Bank; by modeling the kind of thinking and behavior of, say, knowledge sharing and collaborative behavior, as McChrystal did every day in the video briefings he moderated with thousands of Special Ops forces; by telling stories and putting into context the performance challenges an organization faces, so that everyone understands the urgency of change, as Walker of the Ford Foundation did in championing to his people the need to bring social justice to the digital world, or as Mulcahy did, explaining again and again to different employee groups how they could specifically work in new ways to save Xerox.

Successful leaders will also create broad-based cultural expectations for performance behaviors and expectations, to build "one mind." Recall, for example, Mark Benjamin, former president of NCR, who insisted on giving brutally honest but constructive feedback to his direct reports so that those managers could in turn give the same to their people, and so on down the line.

Great leaders synthesize, contextualize, and help create meaning for everyone in their organization. They also infuse the enterprise with the energy and passion to win.

Make *e pluribus unum* your leadership agenda

Throughout this book, we have examined various practices and other elements of leadership, often—for the ease of learning—in an isolated manner. And some of the things we proscribe may seem at odds with each other; for example, the importance of inspiring and motivating people but also not shirking from giving them tough performance feedback; to be relentless in delivering results and near-term performance, but also to embrace future experimentation and opportunities; to be bold and personally courageous but also to step aside sometimes and let others take the lead. We're not the first to suggest that leadership must embrace both/and thinking.

Ultimately you must strive to find—and continuously translate for others—some meaningful and actionable unity among many different pieces of everything you do and see as a leader: different practices, different ideas, and changes in situation between yesterday and today.

In the end, leadership must be an act (to borrow from the motto of the United States) of *e pluribus unum*: "out of many pieces, one overall." You aren't meant to take on the six practices and many steps within them separately. You must combine all the practices to succeed as a leader. But how you combine them is up to you: it will depend on the context of your organization, your skills, and your aspirations. The way you combine them will change by the day and over the long term as you grow as a leader, as you practice, learning and refining as you go.

But leadership is not only an aggregate of creating vision, building strategy, and getting great people on board. As you lead your organization, you are, both implicitly and explicitly, constructing a system of people that reflects you, your values, and your aspirations. Doing so allows you to make, in iconic leader Steve Jobs's term, "a dent in the universe." Recognize that for all it's worth and your leadership practice will become the best way for you to create your impact on the world.

Further Reading

Introduction

What is leadership?

Kotter, John P. "What Leaders Really Do," *Harvard Business Review*, December 2001.

Zaleznik, Abraham. "Managers and Leaders: Are They Different?" *Harvard Business Review*, January 2004.

Chapter 1: Building a Unifying Vision

Heifetz, Ronald, and Donald L. Laurie. "The Work of Leadership," *Harvard Business Review*, December 2001.

Ibarra, Herminia. "Women and the Vision Thing," *Harvard Business Review*, January 2009.

What is a vision?

Collins, Jim, and Jerry I. Porras. "Building Your Company's Vision," *Harvard Business Review*, September–October 1996.

Laws, Kevin. "Successful Startups Don't Make Money Their Primary Mission," HBR.org, July 10, 2015.

Crafting your vision

Arussy, Lior. *Next Is Now: 5 Steps for Embracing Change—Building a Business That Thrives into the Future.* New York: North Star Way Publishing, 2018.

"Creative Job Titles Can Energize Workers," *Harvard Business Review*, May 2016.

Kouzes, James M., and Barry Posner. "To Lead, Create a Shared Vision," *Harvard Business Review*, January 2009.

Chapter 2: Developing a Strategy

Drucker, Peter F. "The Theory of the Business," *Harvard Business Review*, September–October 1994.

Magretta, Joan. "Jim Collins, Meet Michael Porter," *Harvard Business Review*, December 15, 2011.

Defining strategy

Blank, Steve. "Why the Lean Start-Up Changes Everything," *Harvard Business Review*, May 2013.

Lafley, A. G., and Roger Martin. *Playing to Win: How Strategy Really Works*. Boston: Harvard Business Review Press, 2013.

Leinwand, Paul, and Cesare Manardi. "The Coherence Premium," *Harvard Business Review*, June 2010.

Martin, Roger. "How I Knew AOL Time Warner Was Doomed (No, Really!)" HBR.org, November 2, 2010.

McAfee, Andrew, and Mona Ashiya. "Webvan," Case 602-037. Boston: Harvard Business School, rev. May 10, 2006.

McGrath, Rita Gunther, and Ian MacMillan. "Discovery-Driven Planning," *Harvard Business Review*, July–August 1995.

Ovans, Andrea. "What Is Strategy, Again?" HBR.org, May 15, 2015.

Porter, Michael E. "What Is Strategy?" *Harvard Business Review*, November–December 1996.

Porter, Michael E. "The Five Competitive Forces That Shape Strategy," *Harvard Business Review*, January 2008.

Understand your current situation

Christensen, Clayton M., and Joseph L. Bower. "Disruptive Technologies: Catching the Wave," *Harvard Business Review*, January–February 1995.

Christensen, Clayton M., Michael E. Raynor, and Rory McDonald. "What Is Disruptive Innovation?" *Harvard Business Review*, December 2015.

Johnson, Mark, Clayton Christensen, and Henning Kagermann. "Reinventing Your Business Model," *Harvard Business Review*, December 2008.

Develop options for where and how to compete

Ashkenas, Ron. "Are You Really Ready for an Acquisition?" HBR.org, February 6, 2013.

Capron, Laurence, and Will Mitchell. *Build, Borrow, or Buy: Solving the Growth Dilemma*. Boston: Harvard Business Review Press, 2012.

Christensen, Clayton M., et al. "The New M&A Playbook," *Harvard Business Review*, March 2011.

Davenport, Thomas, and Brook Manville. "From the Judgment of Leadership to the Leadership of Judgment: The Fallacy of Heroic Decision Making," *Leader to Leader*, Fall 2012.

Magretta, Joan. *Understanding Michael Porter: The Essential Guide to Competition and Strategy*. Boston: Harvard Business Review Press, 2011.

Marks, Mitchell Lee, Philip Mirvis, and Ron Ashkenas. "Surviving M&A," *Harvard Business Review*, March 2017.

Test options and engage stakeholders

Ashkenas, Ron, and Logan Chandler. "Four Tips for Better Strategic Planning," HBR.org, October 1, 2013.

Davenport, Tom. "How to Design Smart Business Experiments," *Harvard Business Review*, February 2009.

Allocate resources and manage implementation

Collis, David, and Michael G. Rukstad. "Can You Say What Your Strategy Is?" *Harvard Business Review*, April 2008.

Favaro, Ken. "Defining Strategy, Implementation, Execution," HBR.org, March 31, 2015.

Neilson, Gary, Karla Martin, and Elizabeth Powers. "Successful Strategy Execution," *Harvard Business Review*, June 2008.

Chapter 3: Getting Great People on Board

Assembling your leadership team

Fernández-Aráoz, Claudio. "21st-Century Talent Spotting," *Harvard Business Review*, June 2014.

Goleman, Daniel. "What Makes a Leader?" *Harvard Business Review*, January 2004.

Goleman, Daniel, Richard Boyatzis, and Annie McKee. "Primal Leadership: The Hidden Driver of Great Performance," *Harvard Business Review*, December 2001.

Haas, Martine, and Mark Mortensen. "The Secrets of Great Teamwork," *Harvard Business Review*, June 2016.

Coordinating an organization of teams

Ashkenas, Ron, Dave Ulrich, Todd Jick, and Steve Kerr. *The Boundaryless Organization: Breaking the Chains of Organizational Structure.* San Francisco: Jossey-Bass, 2002.

Edmondson, Amy C. "Teamwork on the Fly," *Harvard Business Review*, April 2012.

Katzenbach, Jon R., and Douglas K. Smith. "The Discipline of Teams," *Harvard Business Review*, March–April 1993.

Manville, Brook. "How to Be a Horizontal and Vertical Leader at the Same Time," Forbes.com, June 28, 2017.

McChrystal, Stanley. *Team of Teams: New Rules of Engagement for a Complex World.* New York: Portfolio, 2015.

Ulrich, Dave, Steve Kerr, and Ron Ashkenas. *The GE Work-Out: How to Implement GE's Revolutionary Method for Busting Bureaucracy and Attacking Organizational Problems—Fast!* New York: McGraw-Hill, 2002.

Harnessing performance feedback

Buckingham, Marcus, and Ashley Goodall. "Reinventing Performance Management," *Harvard Business Review*, April 2015.

Cappelli, Peter, and Anna Tavis. "The Performance Management Revolution," *Harvard Business Review*, October 2016.

Krishnamoorthy, Raghu. "The Secret Ingredient in GE's Talent-Review System," HBR.org, April 17, 2014.

Manzoni, Jean-François. "A Better Way to Deliver Bad News," *Harvard Business Review*, September 2002.

Valcour, Monique. "How to Give Tough Feedback That Helps People Grow," HBR.org, August 11, 2015.

Fostering learning and development

Beer, Michael, Magnus Finnström, and Derek Schrader. "Why Leadership Training Fails, and What to Do About It," *Harvard Business Review*, October 2016.

Bellmann, Matthias, and Robert H. Schaffer. "Freeing Managers to Innovate," *Harvard Business Review*, June 2001.

Incentives

Kerr, Steve. "The Best-Laid Incentive Plans," *Harvard Business Review*, January 2003.

Shaping a culture for executing your strategy

Beard, Alison. "CEOs Shouldn't Try to Embody Their Firms' Culture," *Harvard Business Review*, July–August 2016.

Katzenbach, Jon, et al. "Cultural Change That Sticks," *Harvard Business Review*, July–August 2012.

Chapter 4: Focusing on Results

Focusing on results at XL insurance

Sclafane, Susanne. "XL's Seraina Maag: Building a Culture of Collaboration," *Carrier Management*, September 2013.

Setting high performance goals and holding people accountable

Schaffer, Robert H. "Demand Better Results—and Get Them," *Harvard Business Review*, March–April 1991.

Reducing organizational complexity

Ashkenas, Ron. "Simplicity-Minded Management," *Harvard Business Review*, December 2007.

Building capabilities while growing results

Amabile, Theresa, and Steven J. Kramer. "The Power of Small Wins," *Harvard Business Review*, May 2011.

Eisenstat, Russell, Bert Spector, and Michael Beer. "Why Change Programs Don't Produce Change," *Harvard Business Review*, November–December 1990.

Mata, Nadim, and Ron Ashkenas. "Why Good Projects Fail Anyway," *Harvard Business Review*, September 2003.

McGinn, Daniel. "What Companies Can Learn from Military Teams," HBR.org, August 6, 2015.

Schaffer, Robert. "Successful Change Programs Begin with Results," *Harvard Business Review*, January 1992.

Maintaining organizational discipline

Charan, Ram. "You Can't Be a Wimp—Make the Tough Calls," *Harvard Business Review*, November 2013.

Davenport, Thomas H., and Brook Manville. *Judgment Calls: Twelve Stories of Big Decisions and the Teams That Got Them Right*. Boston: Harvard Business Review Press, 2012.

Dewar, Carolyn, and Scott Keller. "Three Steps to a High-Performance Culture," HBR.org, January 26, 2012.

Kaplan, Robert S., and David P. Norton. "The Balanced Scorecard: Measures That Drive Performance," *Harvard Business Review*, July–August 2005.

Kaplan, Robert S., and David P. Norton. "Putting the Balanced Scorecard to Work," *Harvard Business Review*, September–October 1993.

Chapter 5: Innovating for the Future

Collins, Jim, and Jerry Porras. *Built to Last: Successful Habits of Visionary Companies*. New York: HarperCollins, 1994.

Govindarajan, Vijay. "The Scary Truth About Corporate Survival," *Harvard Business Review*, December 2016.

Hoffman, Bryce G. *American Icon: Alan Mulally and the Fight to Save Ford Motor Company*. New York: Crown Publishing, 2012.

Balancing the present and future

Anthony, Scott, Clark Gilbert, and Mark W. Johnson. *Dual Transformation: How to Reposition Today's Business While Creating the Future*. Boston: Harvard Business Review Press, 2017.

Christensen, Clayton M. *The Innovator's Dilemma: When New Technologies Cause Great Firms to Fail*. Boston: Harvard Business School Press, 1995.

Coley, Steve, "Enduring Ideas: The Three Horizons of Growth," *McKinsey Quarterly*, December 2009.

Govindarajan, Vijay. *The Three-Box Solution: A Strategy for Leading Innovation*. Boston: Harvard Business Review Press, 2016.

Govindarajan, Vijay, and Chris Trimble. "The CEO's Role in Business Model Reinvention," *Harvard Business Review*, May 2011.

Schaffer, Robert, and Ron Ashkenas. *Rapid Results: How 100-Day Projects Build the Capacity for Large-Scale Change*. San Francisco: John Wiley & Sons, 2005.

Shaping the future

Birkinshaw, Julian, and Martine Haas. "Increase Your Return on Failure," *Harvard Business Review*, May 2016.

Blank, Steve. "Why the Lean Start-Up Changes Everything," *Harvard Business Review*, May 2013.

Christensen, Clayton, and Michael Overdorf. "Meeting the Challenge of Disruptive Change," *Harvard Business Review*, March–April 2000.

Darling, Marilyn, Charles Parry, and Joseph Moore. "Learning in the Thick of It," *Harvard Business Review*, July–August 2005.

Govindarajan, Vijay. "Planned Opportunism," *Harvard Business Review*, May 2016.

Johnson, Mark. "Reinventing Your Business Model," *Harvard Business Review*, October 2009.

McGrath, Rita, and Ian MacMillan. "Discovery-Driven Planning," *Harvard Business Review*, July–August 1995.

Embracing the future

Barton, Dominic, James Manyika, and Sarah Keohane Williamson. "The Data: Where Long-Termism Pays Off," *Harvard Business Review*, May–June 2017.

Heifetz, Ron, and Donald L. Laurie. "The Work of Leadership," *Harvard Business Review*, December 2001.

Kotter, John. "Leading Change: Why Transformation Efforts Fail," *Harvard Business Review*, January 2007.

Chapter 6: Leading Yourself

Knowing yourself

Craig, Nick, and Scott Snook. "From Purpose to Impact," *Harvard Business Review*, May 2014.

Drucker, Peter F. "Managing Oneself," *Harvard Business Review*, March–April 1999.

George, Bill, Peter Sims, Andrew N. McLean, and Diana Mayer. "Discovering Your Authentic Leadership," *Harvard Business Review*, February 2007.

Goleman, Daniel. "What Makes a Leader?" *Harvard Business Review*, November–December 1998.

Ibarra, Herminia. "The Authenticity Paradox," *Harvard Business Review*, January–February 2015.

Kaplan, Robert S. "What to Ask the Person in the Mirror," *Harvard Business Review*, January 2007.

Growing yourself

Ancona, Deborah, et al. "In Praise of the Incomplete Leader," *Harvard Business Review*, February 2007.

Argyris, Chris. "Teaching Smart People How to Learn," *Harvard Business Review*, May–June 1991.

Ashkenas, Ron. "If Your Boss Tells You to Get a Coach, Don't Panic," *Harvard Business Review*, February 26, 2015.

Ashkenas, Ron, Suzanne Francis, and Rick Heinick. "The Merger Dividend," *Harvard Business Review*, July–August 2011.

Baldoni, John. "Before Working with a Coach, Challenge Your Self-Assumptions," HBR.org, March 15, 2013.

Benko, Cathy, and Molly Anderson. *The Corporate Lattice: Achieving High Performance in the Changing World of Work*. Boston: Harvard Business School Publishing, 2010.

Bennis, Warren, and Robert J. Thomas. "Crucibles of Leadership," *Harvard Business Review*, September 2002.

Edmondson, Amy C. "Strategies for Learning from Failure," *Harvard Business Review*, April 2011.

Goldsmith, Marshall, and Gardiner Morse. "Behave Yourself," *Harvard Business Review*, October 2002.

Kaplan, Robert E., and Robert B. Kaiser. "Stop Overdoing Your Strengths," *Harvard Business Review*, February 2009.

Manville, Brook. "How a Stint in 'Dead-End HR' Made Anne Mulcahy a Better CEO," Forbes.com, April 3, 2016.

Manville, Brook. "Learning in the New Economy," *Leader to Leader* 20 (Spring 2001): 36–45.

Marks, Mitchell Lee, Phillip Mirvis, and Ron Ashkenas. "Rebounding from Career Setbacks," *Harvard Business Review*, October 2014.

Marks, Mitchell Lee, Philip Mirvis, and Ron Ashkenas. "Surviving M&A," *Harvard Business Review*, March–April 2017.

Wenger, Etienne C., and William M. Snyder. "Communities of Practice: The Organizational Frontier," *Harvard Business Review*, January–February 2000.

Sharing yourself

Casciaro, Tiziana, Francesca Gino, and Maryam Kouchaki. "Learn to Love Networking," *Harvard Business Review*, May 2016.

Cross, Rob, Reb Rebele, and Adam Grant. "Collaborative Overload," *Harvard Business Review*, January–February 2016.

Farnell, Richard. "Mentor People Who Aren't Like You," *Harvard Business Review*, April 17, 2017

Finklestein, Sydney. "The Best Leaders Are Great Teachers," *Harvard Business Review*, January–February 2018.

Grant, Adam. "In the Company of Givers and Takers," *Harvard Business Review*, April 2013.

Silver, Nora, and Paul Jansen. "The Multisector Career Arc: The Importance of Cross-Sector Affiliations," *California Management Review*, November 1, 2017.

Taking care of yourself

Ashkenas, Ron. "How Trivial Decisions Will Impact Your Happiness," HBR.org, December 13, 2010.

Christensen, Clayton M. "How Will You Measure Your Life?" *Harvard Business Review*, July–August 2010.

Friedman, Stewart D. "Be a Better Leader, Have a Richer Life," *Harvard Business Review*, April 2008.

Pozen, Robert. "Boring Is Productive," HBR.org, September 19, 2012.

Schwartz, Tony, and Catherine McCarthy. "Manage Your Energy, Not Your Time," *Harvard Business Review*, October 2007.

Seppala, Emma. "How Meditation Benefits CEOs," HBR.org, December 14, 2015.

Index

Acknowledgments

The creation of this book required the help of many people. As such, we owe a collective debt of gratitude to a wide range of friends, colleagues, and generous practitioners who shared their wisdom, helped us get smarter about leadership, and supported us through the journey from rough outline to final production.

The *Leader's Handbook* project began with a brainstorming session between the two of us and our HBR editor, Ania Wieckowski. As the concept developed, Ania went on to become not just an editor, but a true partner. She tirelessly and collaboratively kept us on track through many months, while also diligently challenging us to keep improving the presentation of our ideas. Several of Ania's HBR colleagues also contributed by sharing their perspectives about key trends and enduring tenets of management, as regularly published in the magazine and on the HBR website. Thanks also to Jane Gebhart, whose careful work as our copy editor ensured a higher standard of consistency and quality in the pages that follow, and to Anne Starr, our production editor, who shepherded the manuscript through to completion.

We also want to express our appreciation to several dozen practicing leaders, both entrepreneurs and more established executives, who shared their leadership experiences and insights with us through interviews over the last eighteen months (we list them at the end of this section). Our conversations with these practitioners sharpened our understanding of real-world organizational challenges and enriched our ability to discuss the fundamentals of leadership on which this book has been based. Several of their stories and verbatim reflections appear throughout the chapters, but whether quoted or not, these leaders universally contributed to the development of our thinking about the essential practices of this handbook. We were pleased, as the research unfolded, how often our leader interviews generally affirmed the overall thesis of this book, but we should also add that nothing in its pages is intended to ascribe a specific view of leadership to anyone except ourselves.

We would be remiss if we also did not thank the many clients and organizations that we had the opportunity to work with over the past thirty years of our own consulting and leadership practices. In many ways, this book was a capstone project that allowed us to reflect on and pull together the learning that we accumulated from these collaborations. Some of their stories also are captured in the preceding pages.

It may seem self-serving for coauthors to thank one another, but as a sort of collegial epilogue, we would like to close our collective acknowledgments with gratitude for the value of the collaboration that developed during the course of writing a book together. We began the first draft with a fair amount of conceptual consensus between us, but then had plenty of disagreements and debates along the way. Though sometimes painful, in the end they were, again and again, "learning opportunities." We are each better and wiser for the exchanges that culminated in the final product, and more important, we think this handbook is too.

As coauthors, each of us also would like to note a few personal acknowledgments:

RON: Over the past four decades, colleagues at Schaffer Consulting have deeply influenced my perspective on organizational change and leadership, and supported my professional development. So in many ways, this book is a reflection of what I learned during my time as an active member of the firm. Thanks in particular to Robert Schaffer, who took a chance on me as a naïve would-be consultant and continually encouraged me to keep learning and writing about what it takes for organizations and leaders to be successful. Thanks as well to longtime colleagues Suzanne Francis, Matthew McCreight, Nadim Matta, and others from the firm who were great learning partners over the years. I also wish to acknowledge the many professional colleagues from other firms and universities that I collaborated with on large-scale change projects, postmerger integrations, and previous articles and books. This handbook would not have been possible without the foundation that they provided.

Finally I would like to thank my family for all of their support and understanding while I was preoccupied with the research and writing that went into this book. My adult children (Eliora, Shira, and Ari) and their spouses (Elie, Ben, and Rebecca) continually asked me about the project and cheered me along, despite my having less time for helping out with their growing families or for talking with them about their professional and personal aspirations. Fortunately my wife, Barbara, stepped into the breach and more than made up for my lack of availability. Barbara also encouraged me to keep going whenever I was frustrated or blocked, celebrated with me at key milestones, and provided the steady and loving presence that allowed me to complete this project. As with my other books, I couldn't have done it without her. She is the true leader in our family.

BROOK: I would like to thank colleagues, friends, and family who have, over decades of work in both the for-profit and nonprofit sectors, supported or contributed to my own work on leadership. Too numerous to name are the many professionals with whom, over the years, I have worked and learned about leadership, both as a member of an organization (CBS Inc., McKinsey & Co., Saba Software, United Way Worldwide) and as an adviser and coach to many others as clients. I also gained invaluable insights in recent years from my three adult children (Sabrina, Laura, Martin) and their spouses (Michael, Brian, and Elise)—all of whom are rising leaders in their own professions. They helpfully shared relevant stories from their work experiences with me, which stimulated my thinking; and they variously commented more specifically on parts of our manuscript, which continued to ground me in issues critical for today's early-career professionals. And finally I lovingly thank my wife and life partner, Margarita, whose consistent support and patience with me through many years has enabled me to write now "yet another book."

Leaders Interviewed or Consulted

CAROLINE ANSTEY, senior advisor to the International Development Bank. She was previously a managing director of the World Bank.

DOMINIC BARTON, global managing partner of McKinsey & Co., July 2009–July 2018

MARK BENJAMIN, CEO of Nuance Communications Inc. Previously he was the president and COO of the NCR Corporation.

CHARLIE BROWN, founder and CEO, Context Partners

USHA CHAUDHARY, president and chief operating officer, Kettler

JEANNE CRAIN, president and CEO, Bremer Financial Corporation

PAT DOLAN, vice president of engineering and Boeing military aircraft chief engineer

ROGER W. FERGUSON JR., president and CEO, TIAA

PETER FISHER, senior fellow at the Center for Business, Government, and Society, and clinical professor at the Tuck School of Business at Dartmouth University. Previously he was the head of fixed income portfolio management at BlackRock and the undersecretary for domestic finance in the US Treasury.

YARON GALAI, cofounder and chief executive officer of the digital media startup Outbrain

ANDREW GÉCZY, CEO, Terra Firma Capital Partners Limited

JIM GOODRICH, former director and chief operating officer, McKinsey & Co., 1987–1996

PETER GRIFFITH, global vice chair, corporate development, EY

PAULA KERGER, president and CEO of PBS

JANE KIRKLAND, senior vice president, investment servicing business, State Street Corporation

RICHARD LESSER, president and CEO of the Boston Consulting Group

CHRIS LISCHEWSKI, president and CEO, Bumble Bee Seafoods LLC

JOHN LUNDGREN, formerly CEO and chairman, Stanley, Black & Decker, 2004–2016

TAMARA L. LUNDGREN, president and chief executive officer, Schnitzer Steel Industries, Inc.

RICHARD LYONS, dean of Haas School of Business at the University of California, Berkeley

SERAINA MACIA, executive vice president of AIG and CEO of Blackboard Insurance, a technology-focused subsidiary of AIG. Formerly she was CEO of regional management and operations at AIG and CEO of AIG EMEA. She joined AIG from XL Insurance, where she was chief executive of XL's North American property and casualty business.

KATHERINE MANUEL, senior vice president, innovation, Thomson Reuters

JOHN MARTIN, formerly CEO of Innography, 2013–2017

STANLEY MCCHRYSTAL, US Army (retired), CEO of the McChrystal Group, former commander of the US Joint Special Operations Command, 2003–2008

ANNE MULCAHY, former chairman and CEO of Xerox Corporation, 2001–2010. She retired as chairman in 2010.

RICHARD OBER, president and CEO of the New Hampshire Charitable Foundation

PATRICK O'SULLIVAN, chairman of Saga Plc. He was previously the chairman of Old Mutual Plc, vice chairman of Zurich Financial Services, and CEO of Eagle Star Insurance.

RUNE OLAV PEDERSEN, president and CEO, Petroleum Geo-Services ASA (PGS)

BOB PROCTOR, founding member, Blu Venture Investors, and CEO of Linked Labs

HUNTER R. RAWLINGS III, formerly president of the University of Iowa (1988–1995) and Cornell University (1995–2003), and acting president of Cornell, 2005–2006 and 2016–2017

GARY RODKIN, former CEO of ConAgra Foods, 2005–2015.

MICHAEL ROTH, president of Wesleyan University, Middletown, Connecticut

DAN SPRINGER, CEO of DocuSign. He was previously the chairman and CEO of Responsys.

DARREN WALKER, president, Ford Foundation

DAVID WINN, advisory consultant and former president of American Express Bank, France

MIKE WIRTH, chair and CEO of Chevron Corporation

ANDREW WOLK, founder and CEO, Root Cause

JIM ZIOLKOWSKI, founder and CEO, buildOn

About the Authors

RON ASHKENAS has been a thought partner, consultant, and coach on organizational change, leadership, and transformation with prominent private, nonprofit, and public-sector executives for over thirty years and is an Emeritus Partner of Schaffer Consulting in Stamford, Connecticut. He was part of the team that worked with Jack Welch to transform GE in the 1990s. His other clients have included the World Bank and Federal Reserve Bank of New York; Merck, Pfizer, and GSK pharmaceuticals; technology companies such as Cisco and Cognizant; Stanford Hospital and the MD Anderson Cancer Center; financial services companies such as AIG, JP Morgan Chase, Thomson Reuters, and Zurich Insurance; and consumer products firms including PepsiCo, ConAgra Foods, and P&G.

Ron has written numerous articles for the *Harvard Business Review* and is the author of *Simply Effective: How to Cut Through Complexity in Your Organization and Get Things Done* (Harvard Business Press, 2009). He also is the coauthor of four other books, including *The Boundaryless Organization* and *The GE Work-Out*. He lectures on change management, acquisition integration, simplification, executive leadership, and innovation at universities and conferences worldwide.

BROOK MANVILLE serves as an adviser and executive coach to a wide range of leaders on issues of strategy, organizational development, and leadership effectiveness. Earlier in his career, he served as executive vice president of the United Way of America and chief learning officer at Saba, a Silicon Valley provider of human capital management solutions. As a partner at McKinsey & Company, Brook consulted to several *Fortune*

500 companies, specializing in organizational development and knowledge-related strategy. He was also McKinsey's first director of knowledge management.

Brook is a regular contributor to the Leadership Channel in Forbes.com. In addition to *Harvard Business Review*, he has written for *Fast Company* and *Sloan Management Review* and is the author (with Josiah Ober) of *A Company of Citizens: What the World's First Democracy Teaches Leaders About Creating Great Organizations* (Harvard Business School Press, 2003) and (with Tom Davenport) *Judgment Calls: Twelve Stories of Big Decisions and the Teams That Got Them Right* (Harvard Business Review Press, 2012).

The most important management ideas all in one place.

We hope you enjoyed this book from *Harvard Business Review*. For the best ideas HBR has to offer turn to HBR's 10 Must Reads Boxed Set. From books on leadership and strategy to managing yourself and others, this 6-book collection delivers articles on the most essential business topics to help you succeed.

HBR's 10 Must Reads Series

The definitive collection of ideas and best practices on our most sought-after topics from the best minds in business.

- Change Management
- Collaboration
- Communication
- Emotional Intelligence
- Innovation
- Leadership
- Making Smart Decisions

- Managing Across Cultures
- Managing People
- Managing Yourself
- Strategic Marketing
- Strategy
- Teams
- The Essentials

hbr.org/mustreads

Buy for your team, clients, or event.
Visit hbr.org/bulksales for quantity discount rates.